# PREPARATION, TRY OUT AND STUDY OF EFFECTIVENESS OF A PSYCHOLOGICAL EDUCATION PROGRAMME ON HIGH SCHOOL STUDENTS BASED ON WILLIAM GLASSER'S REALITY THERAPY

RITA ROY

# A C K N O W L E D G E M E N T

The investigator wishes to express her deep and sincere indebtedness to Dr. V.D.Thomas, her Ph.D. guide for his kind and valuable guidance and constant inspiration throughout her Ph.D. work.

The investigator also likes to express her thanks to the Head of the Department of the "Centre of Advanced Study in Education" Dr.Sunirmal Roy, and to all the teachers and well-wishers of the Centre who had lent their constant help in all matters during the course of her study.

The investigator wishes to express her special gratitude to Mrs.Saroj Padhye Librarian, Centre of Advanced Study in Education and to the staffs of Smt.Hansa Mehta Library - Baroda, Documentation Library-Baroda, United States Educational Foundation in India-Culcutta, National library-Calcutta, British Council library-Calcutta, Vinay-Bhawan-library-Santiniketan and also to The Institute of Reality Therapy California U.S.A. and to the American Psychological Association, Washington, U.S.A.

Investigator

*Rita Roy*
(Rita Roy)
September, 1995
Baroda

Centre of Advanced Study in Education
M.S. University
Baroda.

# CONTENTS

Acknowledgements

# List of Tables

2

4

1

# CHAPTER - I

## EDUCATION, PSYCHOLOGICAL EDUCATION, REALITY THERAPY

### 1.1 Introduction :

The present study deals with "Reality Therapy" - a psychological education program in schools. In order to properly situate the study and Reality Therapy in the context of education, the investigator has attempted to start this research report with a brief account of the concept of education itself.

### 1.2 Concept of education :

Since the word "education" is used in so many ways, the concept of education is much difficult to define. Different educational thinkers have given different definitions of education in different ages. From all these definitions one could find out what education means to different persons and how its meaning had been altered from time to time, from society to society and from culture to culture.

Plato wrote, "By education I mean that training which is given by stable habits to the first instincts of virtue in children when pleasure and pain are rightly implanted in non-rational souls. The practical training in respect of pleasure and pain which leads you to hate and love, what you ought to hate and love is called education." (Plato, Republic 1945)

Russell defined education as follows, "I call therefore a complete and generous education that which fits a man to perform justly, skillfully, and magnanimously all the offices both public and private of peace and war". (B.Russell - Education and the good life 1926)

Lodge wrote "Education is equivalent to experience — the experience of a living organisms interacting with its normal environment." (Lodge, R. — Philosophy of Education 1937 ) According to Horne, "Education is the eternal process of superior adjustment of the physically and mentally developed free conscious human being to God as manifested in the intellectual, emotional and vocational environment of man." (Horne, Herman — The democratic Philosophy of Education, 1935)

Langford suggested, "Education is an activity which aims at theoretical results". (Feeling & Form, 1953)

Sometimes one also speaks of life itself as being educational and in this sense one usually has in mind the idea that if school room activities are educational then there are many similar ones taking place outside the school that have the same kind of impluence on us.

Education in this sense designates the broader process whereby we come to accept the goals and values of our society and for this we can talk of education as being a lifelong process ( Hopkins 1941 )

Again we can say that the term 'education' designates that basic social process whereby individuals acquires the culture of their society, we call this the process of socialisation, which is acquired through both formal and informal means.

But education is also equivalent to socialisation and in this sense it is a wholly conservative process. This conception has always been criticised and attacked be cause it provides no wider goals for men.

Western civilisation has developed a third level of meaning for the term "education", that is adaptation with the
environment. According to this view some degree of adaptability
to varying circumstances must occur if it is to survive.

Besides all the above mentioned views there are various
view-points about education and the learned people differ among
themselves to come to a precise definition of education.

For example :-

- Is education the process of drawing out of children, ideas
  that lie implicitly imbedded in their minds ?

- Is it the process of developing abilities that are innately
  part of everyone's human nature ?

- Is it the process of activating the brain so as to acquire
  record and store organized bodies of fact and value ?

- Is it the process of writing and rewriting social experience on the "tabuls Rasa" of the individual ?

- Is it the process of raising children to adjust to and
  live in a certain kind of society ?

These questions though they have different conceptions,
imply the following conclusion.

First, education cannot be all of these things, because the
above mentioned views are contradictory and they cannot exist
with each other to give an adequate definition of education.

Secondly, whatever education may or may not be, it is
evidently a process.

Thirdly, a more careful inspection of these alternatives reveal atleast three basic approaches to the process of education. They are :-

a)   Education as manifestation
b)   Education as acquisition
c)   Education as transaction.

a)   Education as manifestation :

According to this view Education is the process of making manifest what is latent in each child (Brauner, 1964) Those who adhere to this view believe that education can be described as an analogy to the growth and development of flowers in which the latent potentialities of the seed bloom into the manifested splendor of the mature flower. Analogically the child is the seed in which all the unrealized potentialities lie dormant, the teacher is the gardener whose tender loving care will help to unfold these hidden promises and education is the teaching of gardening process by which these unseen capacities will become visible through the judicious choice of fertilizers.

b)   Education as acquisition :

This approach to education places more emphasis on the ability of man to acquire information by inquiry into the nature of the external world (Cowley 1957). Here inquiry is more a process of taking in what exists outside then learner, rather than a process of bringing out what exists internally in him.

This school believes that the brain of the child like a sponge never completely dries out, for it exists in a world that is constantly spraying it with drops of information.

c)   Education as Transaction :

A third view sees education as transaction (Scheffler, 1960),
the process of give and take between man and his environment. Through this process, man develops the skills needed
to modify and improves the conditions of his environment
and which guides his efforts in guiding and reconstructuring
the human as well as physical nature.

1.3  The Goal of Education :

However, the goal of the education from society's view point
then is the production of adequate person - people who can be
counted upon to behave effectively and efficiently and to
contribute freely to the welfare of all.

The term adequate person may be defined as one who :-

a)   perceives himself in essentially positive ways.
b)   is open to his experience and capable of accepting
     self and others.
c)   is strongly and broadly identified with others.

These perceptual characteristics of adequate persons define
more specifically the goal of education. An adequate educational
system which produces these kinds of perceptual characteristics
in its students is successful. A system which fails to affect
these important criteria has no doubt failed.

Therefore  the broad purpose of education is to facilitate
the integration of a student's total personality in such a way
as to maximize knowledge and skill development for productive
living.

When we educate students we help them to develop their own
unique personalities by bringing out their ideas and feelings
into communication with others, breaking down the barriers that
produce isolation in a world where for their own mental health
and physical well-being they must learn to be a part of the
human race ( Rogers, 1961 ).

Similarly Hopkins (1941) advanced the idea that education
is a continuous and lifelong process and should therefore also
be concerned with life coping skills not just the classroom or
academic subjects isolated from the larger world.

Therefore it seems reasonable to help students to develop
the skills necessary for establishing and maintaining an
effective interpersonal relationship.

Clearly our schools have a tremendous important role to
perform in our culture. Unfortunately, we have not always
provided our teachers with the proper training that would help
to ensure the development of adequate personality in the students'
best interest. However in considering where to concentrate our
efforts at creating a healthier society, psychological education
is emerging as a potential force in the schools. The main
purpose of psychological education is to use classroom situations
as a means for promoting personal growth and development.

More specifically, psychological education :-

a)   Accepts the learners' needs and purposes and develops
     experiences and programs around the unique potential of
     the learner.

b)   facilitates self-actualization and strives to develop a
     sense of personal adequacy.

c)  fosters acquisition of basic skills necessary for living
    in a multicultural society including academic, personal,
    interpersonal, communicative and economic proficiency.

d)  personalizes educational decisions and practices.

e)  recognizes the primacy of human feelings, personal values
    and perceptions as integral factors in educational processes.

f)  develops a learning climate that is challenging, under-
    standing, supportive exciting and free from threat.

g)  develops in learners genuine concern and respect for the
    worth of others and skill in conflict resolutions.

The programmes of psychological education promise to meet
all these demands.

Having inquired into the concept of education in general
and psychological education in particular, we may turn our
attention to one of the prominent form of Psychological Education Program prevalent especially in the American schools,
namely the Reality Therapy of Dr.William Glasser.

## 1.4 Reality Therapy - its nature and concept :

Reality Therapy was developed by Dr.William Glasser who
founded the Institute for Reality Therapy in Los Angeles,
California (U.S.A.) in 1967. He believes that all people are
born with atleast two built in needs.

a)  The need to belong and to love.
b)  The need to compete for worth and recognition.

According to Glasser, we spend our lives struggling to satisfy
these needs and when we can't, we suffer. Through a series of
well defined steps  Reality Therapists teach people who struggle
unsuccessfully to satisfy these needs more effectively.

## 1.5  History and Development :

When Dr. Glasser finished Western Reserve University Medical
School in Cleveland Ohio (U.S.A.) in 1953 and later in his
psychiatric residency in Los Angeles, he had been taught that
the psychiatric patients were the victims of people and events
beyond their control.  To help them he would have to deal exten-
sively with their past and concentrate on how they feel about
those events.

His early work was in a California School for delinquent
girls, the Ventuara School, where he learned quickly that unless
he developed a better way to help these girls to deal with the
world, they would probably return, With G.L. Harrington he
developed the ideas which soon came to be known as Reality
Therapy.  A detailed description of the development of this
therapy can be found in Glasser's book "Reality Therapy - a new
approach to psychiatry". (1965) N.York Harper & Row.

Since then Glasser and those he has trained have taught
Reality Therapy to people working in every possible therapeautic
situation- individual and group therapy, school counseling,
rehabilitation, correction, Mental hospitals and others specific
cases showing the diversity of the use of Reality Therapy, and
are described in the book "What are you doing" (1980, Glasser).
It shows how the basic theory has been applied not only to
widely diverse individuals but also to entire programs such as
schools, correctional facilities, and mental hospitals.

There is example that entire school districts have trained personnel to understand, teach and discipline their students following Glasser's book "School without failure".

The detailed description of the therapeutic process of Reality Therapy is as under.

1.6  The Therapeutic Process of Reality Therapy :

a.  Therapeutic Goals :  The overall goal of Reality Therapy is for individuals to find more effective ways of meeting their needs for belonging power, freedom and fun. At his workshop Glasser stresses that counseling consists of helping clients to learn ways to regain control of their lives and to live more effectively. This includes confronting clients to examine what they are doing, thinking and feeling to figure out if there is a better way for them to function.

Reality Therapy focuses on what clients are conscious of and then to increase their level of awareness. All clients become aware of the ineffective behaviours they are using to control the world, they are more open to learning alternative ways of behaviour. Unlike many other approaches, Reality Therapy is concerned with teaching people these more effective ways to deal with the world. The core of Reality Therapy is to help clients to evaluate whether their wants are realistic and whether their behaviour is helping them. It is the clients who decide if what they are doing is getting them what they want and they determine what changes if any they are willing to make. After they make this assessment they are

assisted by the counselor *who* designing a plan for
change as a way of translating talk into action.
Glasser (1989) emphasizes that the only person's
behaviour that we can control is our own which means
that the best way to control events around us is
through we do.

b.    Therapist's function and Role :  The reality therapist's job is to get involved with clients and to
develop a relationship with them that will lay the
groundwork for the rest of the counseling process.
The counselor functions as a teacher by being active
in the sessions, helping clients to formulate
specific plans of actions offering them behavioural
choices and teaching them control theory. Therapist
challenge clients with the basic question of Reality
Therapy.

Is what you are choosing to do getting you what you want.

If the clients make the judgement that what they are doing
is not working, therapist may suggest an alternative course of
action (William Glasser 1989).  The counselor also teaches
clients how they  can create a success identity by recognizing
and accepting accountability for their own chosen behaviours
(Glasser, 1986).  This role requires counselor to perform
several functions.

a)    providing a model for responsible behaviour and for
a life based on a success identity.

b)    establishing rapport based on care and respect.

c)    focusing on the individual's strengths and potentials
that can lead to success.

d)  actively promoting discussion of client's current
    behaviour and discouraging excuses for irresponsible
    or ineffective behaviour.

e)  introducing and fostering the process of evaluating
    realistically attainable wants.

f)  teaching clients to formulate and carry out plans to
    change their behaviours.

g)  establishing a structure and limits for the sessions.

h)  helping clients find ways to meet their needs and
    refusing to give up easily even if clients become
    discouraged.

c.  Application - Therapeutic techniques and Procedures:

    The practice of Reality Therapy can best be conceptu-
    alized as the cycle of counseling which consists of
    two major components.

    a)  The counseling environment and
    b)  The specific procedures that lead to changes in
        behaviour.

d.  The Counseling Environment: Personal involvement with
    the Client :  The practice of Reality Therapy begins
    with the counselor's efforts to create a supportive
    environment within which clients can begin to make
    changes in their lives. To create this therapeutic
    climate counselor must become involved in the clients'
    lives and establish rapport. This involvement occurs
    through a combined process of listening to the clients'
    story and skillfully questioning.

12

e.  Counselor's attitudes and behaviours that promote change :

Counselor consistently attempts to focus clients on what
they are doing now.  They also avoid discussing client's
feelings or physiology as though these were seperate from
their total behaviour.  Counselors help their clients to
see connections between what they are feeling and their
concurrent actions and thoughts.  Although Reality Therapists  focus on the actions and thoughts of clients they
consider it quite legitimate to talk about feelings and
physiology.  When people begin to act differently they
also begin to feel differently.  Counselors hope to teach
their clients to value the attitude of accepting responsibility for their total behaviour.  Thus they accept no
excuses for irresponsible behaviour, even though they
recognize that ineffective behaviour is still the client's
best attempt to get what is wanted.  If clients do not
follow through with their agreed plans for change,
counselors are likely to help them reassess the situation,
yet they are firm in their refusals to accept excuses.
Reality Therapists show clients that excuses are a form of
self-deception that may offer temporary relief but ultimately leads to failure.  By refusing to accept excuses
counselors convey their belief in the clients' ability to
regain control.  Reality Therapy holds that punishment is
not useful means of changing behaviour.  Instead of being
punished individuals can learn to accept the reasonable
consequences that follow from their actions.  By not making
critical comments by refusing to accept excuses and by
remaining nonjudgemental, counselors are in a position to
ask the clients if they are really interested in changing.

f.  **Procedures that lead to change: Exploring wants needs and perception** :  In this phase Reality Therapists ask "What do you want ?  Through the therapist's skillful questioning clients are encouraged to recognize, define and refine how they wish to meet their needs.  Part of counseling consists of the exploration of their picture album and the ways in which their behaviour is aimed at moving their perception of the external world closer to their inner world of wants. The skill of Reality Therapy involves counseling in a noncriticizing and accepting way so that clients will reveal what is in their special world.  Clients are given the opportunity to explore every facet of their lives, including what they want from their family friends and work.  Furthermore, it is useful for them to define what they expect and want from the counselor and from themselves (Wubbolding 1988).

This exploration of wants needs and perceptions should continue throughout the counseling process because the client's pictures change.  After clients explore their picture album they are later asked to look at their behaviour to determine if what they are doing is getting them what they want.

g.  **Focus on current Behaviour** :  Reality Therapy stresses current behaviour and is concerned with past event only in so far as they influence how the client is behaving now. The focus on the present is characterized by the question so often asked by the reality therapist what are you doing? Even though problems may be rooted in the past clients need to learn how to deal with them in the present by learning better ways of getting what they want.  Glasser (1989) contends that no matter how frustrating the past was, there is way through which either the client or the therapist can undo these frustrations. What can be done now is to help clients make more need satisfying choices.

14

Reality Therapy concentrates on changing current total
behaviour, not mere attitudes & feelings. That doesn't imply
that attitudes are dismissed as unimportant, rather total
behavioural change is easier to effect than attitudinal change
and it is of great value in the therapeutic process. For that
reason a client who expressed feelings of helplessness would
not be questioned about the reasons for the feelings but would
be encouraged to describe a time when he was not helpless.
What was he doing then that is different from what he is doing
now.

Although the Reality Therapist might encourage the client
to discuss feelings, the focus would be clearly on the acting
and thinking part of the total behavioural system. The therapist would urge the person to identify those thoughts and
actions that accompanied the feelings. The aim is to help
clients understand their responsibilities for their own feelings : Questions such as the following are likely to be asked.

- What are you doing now ?
- What did you actually do this past week ?
- What did you want to do differently this past week ?
- What stopped you from doing what you say you want
  to do ?
- What will you do tomorrow ?

Listening to clients talk about feelings can be productive but
only if it is linked to what they are doing.

When clients talk about problems-feelings the counselor
rather than focusing on these feelings needs to encourage them
to take action by changing what they are doing and thinking.
According to Glasser (1980,81,85,89) what we are doing is easy

to see and impossible to deny and thus it serves as the proper
focus in the therapy. Discussions centering on feeling without
strongly relating them to what people are doing are counter-
productive (Glasser 1980) Briefly then the focus of Reality Therapy is on gaining awareness of current total behaviour because
this process contributes in helping a person get what he or she
wants and to develop a positive self image.

h.   Getting Clients to Evaluate their Behaviour :

Asking clients to evaluate each component of their total
behaviour is a major task in Reality Therapy. When therapists
ask a depressing client, if this behaviour is helping in the
long run, they introduce the idea of choice to the client. The
process of evaluation of the doing thinking feeling and physio-
logical components of total behaviour is within the scope of
the client's responsibility. From the reality therapist's
perspective it is acceptable to be directive with certain
clients at the beginning of the treatment. This is done to help
them recognize that some behaviours are not effective. In working with clients who are in crisis, it is sometimes necessary
to suggest straight forwardly what will work and what will not.
Other clients need direction early in the course of treatment
such as alcoholics and children of alcoholics, for they often
do not have the thinking behaviour in their control, to be able
to make consistent evaluations of when their lives are seriously
out of effective control. These clients are likely to have
blurred pictures and at times not to be aware of what they want
or whether their wants are realistic. As they grow and continually interact with the counselor they learn to make the
evaluations with less help from the counselor (Wubbolding 1988)
Some clients insist that they don't have a problem and that
their behaviour is not getting them into trouble. It is essential

to recognize that clients behave according to their perceptions.
Counseling can't be successful unless the counselor can accept
that what the client perceives may be far different from what
the counselor and other who are close to the client may see
(Glasser, 1986). In such cases Glasser (1986) suggests that
counselor should then continue to focus on the client's present
behaviours through the process of skillful questioning. He says
that patience is important, for difficult clients may take
considerable time to realize that certain behaviour pattern are
not getting them what they want and that their behaviour is not
taking them in a direction they want to go.

i.    Planning and Commitment :  Once clients determine what
they want to change, they are generally ready to explore
possible behaviours and formulate an action plan. After plans
have been formulated by a joint effort between the counselor
and the client a commitment must be made to carry them out.
Much of the significant work of counseling consists of helping
clients identity specific ways to fulfill their wants. The
process of creating and carrying out plans is how people gain
control over their lives. This is clearly the teaching phase
of counseling which is best directed toward providing clients
with new information and helping them find more effective ways
of getting what they want. The purpose of the plan is to
arrange for successful experiences. Throughout this planning
phase the counselor continually urges clients to assume
responsibility for their own choices and actions. This is done
by reminding them that no one in the world will do things for
them or live their life for them. Wubbolding (1988) devoted a
full chapter to planning & commitment explaining that clients
gain more effective control over their lives with plans that
have the following characteristics.

(a) The plan should be within the limits of the motivation and capacities of each client. Skillful counselors help members identify plans that involve greater need fulfilling payoffs.

(b) Good plans are simple and easy to understand. Although they need to be specific, concrete and measurable, they should be flexible and open to modification as clients gain a deeper understanding of the specific behaviours that they want to change.

(c) Plans should be realistic and attainable. Counselors can help clients recognize that even small plans will help them take significant steps towards their desired changes. The plan should involve a positive action & it should be used in terms of what the client is willing to do.

(d) Counselors should encourage clients to develop plans that they can carry out independently of what others do. Plans that are contingent on others lead clients to sense that they are not steering their own ship but are at the mercy of the ocean.

(e) Effective plans are repetitive and ideally are performed daily. For example clients can choose to take the initiative by approaching others first to achieve something to have fun and to act independently.

(f) Plans should be carried out as soon as possible. Counselors can ask questions as what are you willing to do to day to begin to change your life ?

   The client may say that he would like to stop depressing. What are you going to do now to attain this goal.

(g)  Effective planning involves process centered activities.
For example clients may plan to do any of the following.

a)   Apply for a job.
b)   Write a letter to a friend.
c)   Take a yoga class  etc.

Before clients carry out their plan, it is a good idea for
them to evaluate it with their therapist to determine if it is
realistic and attainable and if it relates to what they need
and want.

After the plan has been carried out in real life it is
useful to evaluate it again.  The counselor needs to ask :-

Is your plan helpful ?

If a plan does not work it can be reevaluated and alternatives can be considered.  In order for clients to commit
themselves to their plan, it is useful for them to firm it up
in writing.

Resolutions and plans are empty unless there is a commitment to carry them out.  It is up to each client to determine
ways of taking these plans outside the restricted world of
therapy and into the every day world.  Effective therapy can be
the catalyst that leads to self-directed responsible living.

## 1.7 Special Procedures in Reality Therapy :

Four special procedures that can be appropriately used to augment the practice of Reality Therapy are :-

   a.   The skillful use of questioning.
   b.   Self-help techniques for a personal growth plan.
   c.   The use of humor, and
   d.   Paradoxical techniques.

(a)   The art of skillfull questioning : Because Reality Therapy uses questioning to a greater degree than many other approaches, counselors need to develop extensive questioning skills.

   Four main purposes for questioning procedures are :-

   a)   To enter the inner world of the client.
   b)   To gather information.
   c)   To give information.
   d)   To help clients take more effective control of their lives (Wubbolding 1988).

Questioning is often misused by counselors especially those who are inexperienced. Closed questions or ones that simply tap information can be overdone and tend to result in defensiveness and resistance. Open questions that are well timed, however, can lead clients to think about what they want and to evaluate whether their behaviour is leading them in the direction they want to go.

(b)   Self-help procedures for a Personal growth program -
   Wubbolding describes his version of an approach to personal growth in his replacement program. This program helps clients to identify specific need fulfilling wants as well as targets

for change. Replacements include do it behaviours in place of give up behaviours and positive symptom behaviours instead of negative symptom behaviours, key questions help clients focus on what they are doing and thinking and how they are feeling. Strategic questions can have the effect of getting clients to identify specific ways in which they can replace a failure identity with a positive identity.

(c) The use of humor : Several practioners have written about the role that fun and humor have in Reality Therapy. Therapetic humor has an educative corrective message and it helps clients to put situations in perspective. Such humor does not involve hostility, ridicule or lack of respect.

(d) Using Paradoxical Techniques : Clients in Reality Therapy are generally encouraged to change by direct and straightforward procedure. Yet there are times when clients seems especially resistant to making plans or if they do make plans, they may be resistant in carrying them out. Paradoxical techniques place clients in a double bind so that therapeutic change occurs regardless of the paradoxical directives. Clients may be asked to exaggerate a problematic behaviour. Clients who complain that they can't sleep, are directed to attempt to say awake. By accepting the therapist's directives and thus maintaining the symptom, clients demonstrate control over it and are no longer helpless. And if clients choose to resist the directive and let go of a particular symptom, the behaviour is not merely controlled but eliminated. Paradoxical procedures are usually not used until the more conventional procedures of Reality Therapy have been tried.

## 1.8 Reality Therapy Programmes in School :

Glasser's book "Schools without failure" present an understandable way to apply the idea of Reality Therapy to Schools. Published in 1967, it was the largest selling American book on education during the 1970's. Enthusiasm from educators who were using the ideas of Reality Therapy helped Glasser to found the Educator Training Centre in 1968 to teach how to use the concepts in school. Starting with the educational films and inservice Training programme - The Educator Training Centre has expanded until the staffs now help universities. For example the University of Wisconsin of La Crosse offers Master degree on these concepts.

At least 300,000 teachers in the U.S.A. have been specifically trained by the Educator Training Centre and countless others have taken courses by those who have had this training.

The Educator Training Centre has developed programs which help school personnel to help students and involve them in their learning in a way that helps them to accept responsibility for their behaviour.

Schools which have applied this program report decreases in suspension by 50-80% in junior and senior high schools and vandalism by 40-90%. Improvement in teacher morale and professional growth was also cited as being significant gains by schools.

The implementation of this program can be further understood by reading a book by a principal, Bill Borger's (1979) "Return to Discipline" who applied the principles of Reality Therapy to the students, teachers and counselors in his school.

He found that by having everone understood how to help students take responsibility for their own behaviours, school could function in a way that produced more learning.

## 1.9 Criticism of Reality Therapy :

The critiques however did not fail to criticize this therapy. One group argued that this therapy has considerable weaknesses because it attempts to describe the condition of all children in all urban schools rather than focusing on specific types, cases or clearly described student population. They added that the examples of negative school experience are cognate but not necessarily ubiquitous. It was the critiques opinion that most curriculum theorists would agree with some of the criticism of education cited but no evidence is given to support the contention that success will automatically follow if Glasser's teaching strategies are adopated.

The critiques argued that Dr.Glasser had ignored much of what social scientists describe in various Theories of identity, anxiety, perception and motivation. Major curriculum innovations have been ignored in Glasser's Therapy. Fenton's History programme, Hanvey's anthropology programme, Oliver's controversial issue project and Taba's teaching strategies are nowhere to be found in his therapy. Many will find some of his own thoughts about the problems of education expressed in his books, the professionals on the other hand will question the stated etiology of school failure and will be disappointed with the lack of evidence in support.

The critiques thought that the solution which Dr.Glasser proposes offer very little hope to anyone who wants to believe that his impossible dream will be obtained.

The critiques also disagreed with Glasser in his general denial of the significance of the past in understanding behaviour in the present. One critique argued "I do not believe in the game of archaeology or digging in the past, but neither do I believe that, we can totally ignore the past. To me the man who ignores his past is like the one who stands in the rain, arguing about its wetness, while becoming drenched". ( Thomas Harris 1969)

In answer to that Glasser states "We do not get involved with the patient's history because we can neither change what happened to him or accept the fact that he is limited by his past".

Critiques argued that it is true we can not change the past. Yet the past invariably, insinuates itself into our present life.

Critiques also argued that Glasser has not provided answer to what is wrong with people who cannot perceive reality or whose perception is distorted. What is the answer to those who know what they must do but continually fail to do it ?

Another reservation about Reality Therapy is that it does not have a special language with which to report what happened. Glasser states 'the ability of the therapist to get involved is the major skill of doing Reality Therapy but it is most difficult to describe. How does one put into the words the building of a strong emotional relationship quickly between two relative strangers.

According to the critiques Glasser's insistence on a firm commitment would seemingly limit the number of students with whom this approach can be used. Many of the trouble-some

students find their misbehaviour very rewarding and are therefore not inclined to make commitment to change their ways.
Others have already turned out because of early failure
experiences. Commitments does not come easily for such young-
sters for they have reached the point where they no longer care.

Another criticism about Reality Therapy is that as valuable
as class meetings can be, many teachers feel uncomfortable in
conducting class meeting. Some teachers are too authoritarian
to use this approach effectively. Other simply lacks the skill
required in getting meetings underway and in keeping them
going in meaningful ways. Still others are afraid that class
meetings will give the student too much power and that they
will then take over the class.

But taking into consideration all the above mentioned
views one must admit that Reality therapy is a straightforward
approach that has considerable appeal. Its stress on the
development of personal responsibility, its concern with the
child's problems in the real world, its teaching of children
to use their brains in the solution of social problems and
its reliance on logic and behaviour rather than insight will
definitely earn this approach high marks from the practitioner.

## 1.10 Rationale of the study :

Psychological education programme which aims at developing personal aspects of students is totally absent from the
Indian educational scene. There is a dire need to introduce
such programmes in school education. Today it is emerging as
a potent force in the schools and colleges. The main purpose
of the present study which is nothing but a psychological
education programme is to use the classroom as a means of

promoting personal growth and development. Reality Therapy is
nothing but a way of integrating learning about oneself into
education systematically - which is an urgent need of the day.
In a world that is changing so fast - our well being and
effectiveness will depend on how well we are able to relate,
communicate understand ourselves and others. Reality Therapy
is a way to this goal. When the learning climate is one of
acceptance of the learners, as he is and his needs for
security and self-esteem are satisfied he can explore new
avenues of growth and drive for self-actualization. Reality
Therapy contributes to the awakening of interest in the
neglected aspects of education. The investigator personally
feels that Reality Therapy has great impact on the emotional
and personal life of the adolescent students.

With these ideas in mind the investigator wanted to use
this therapy practically on groups of school students and
tried to find out how far this therapy is effective in the
context of Indian educational scene.

### 4.11 The present study :

The present study is on a psychological education programme based on Dr.William Glasser's Reality Therapy, is a
comprehensive approach to organise psychological education in
the classroom and to study the impact of Reality Therapy on
some selected variables both cognitive and affective. The
study is titled as "Preparation, Tryout and study of effectiveness of a Psychological Education Programme on High School
students based on William Glasser's Reality Therapy".

1.12 Limitation of the study :

It is not possible for a researcher to study a set of
phenomena at all a levels and from all possible angles in a
time bound research. Limitations of time and resources compels
every researcher to delimit his/her research endeavour in
respect of scope and level at which the study is ultimately
conducted and the present study is no exception, and it has
been delimited on the following aspects.

a)    The study will be limited to only a small sample of
      students. To her knowledge, the present investigator is
      the first person who has introduced Reality Therapy in the
      Indian school system. Therefore she will introduced this
      programme on a small number of students and if it proves
      effective for the Indian students it can be introduced
      on a large scale.

b)    The study was restricted to three English medium schools
      of Baroda. Again, the investigator took a small number
      of students from each school for the cause mentioned above
      and conducted the same study in the three schools.

c)    It will be restricted to the students who have learning
      & other behavioural problem.

d)    It will be restricted to the standard IX students. The
      investigator had no option in this regard she had to
      depend totally on school principals' opinion on the
      availability of students.

CHAPTER : II

RELATED RESEARCH STUDIES

## 2.0 Introduction :

The present investigation is an intervention study in the area of psychological education employing Reality Therapy. The concepts and nature of psychological education as well as Reality Therapy have been discussed in the previous chapter. In this chapter a short report of some research attempts in the area of psychological education and Reality Therapy in particular are presented.

It may be mentioned in the beginning that Reality Therapy is a very recent development in the field of education and psychology. Researches in this area are yet to pick up. As far as the investigator's knowledge goes she has not found Research Studies on Reality Therapy in India.

Therefore in the first part of this chapter, the investigator has reviewed research studies on a few related variables, such as Assertiveness sense of responsibility, educational aspiration, academic achievement, self-concept and attitude toward school.

In the second part of the chapter she has reviewed researches on Reality Therapy which has been done abroad.

## 2.1 Assertiveness :

Assertive behaviour has been defined differently in various studies to reflect particular deficits. Yet certain aspects of assertiveness are fairly well agreed upon. For example standing up for one's rights, refusing to comply with seemingly unreasonable demands of others and generally expressing feelings overtly to others(both positive and negative feelings)

Psychologists have pointed out that being assertive is a skill that one can learn. In fact assertive behaviour probably is learned early in one's family. It can be trained and developed just as any other social behaviour.

Assertion Theory is based on the assumption that everyone has basic human rights which should be respected and that assertion skills could be developed. The theory of assertion emphasises the basic rights that we all have and the responsibilities which go with having these rights. Some important research studies on assertiveness in the Indian field of education are as follows :-

S.C. Saxena (1987) studied the leadership qualities of students and found that middle school leaders, that is, those who take leading roles in all school activities were asertive.

S.Khan (1983) in his study opposed the popular belief and came to the conclusion that educationally backward students are more assertive. Their lack of self confidence in the field of education do not hinder them to become assertive.

S. Malik (1984) found that popular adolescent students are more assertive than their unpopular counterparts.

P. Sukumaran (1982) also conducted research on adolescent boys and found that they are generally more assertive.

M. Panda (1983) concluded that father's locus of control was negatively related to son's assertiveness.

V. Datta (1981) made a study of assertiveness in Inter-mediate students and found that higher intelligence made subjects comprehend things and situation better resulting in greater confidence and decreased submission.

K. Bose (1960) made research on the living pattern of the adolescents and its effect on their character and came to the conclusion that boys living in crowded houses without facilities of a comfortable and peaceful life are self-assertive.

R.K. Mishra (1968) studied certain personality correlates of Need for achievement and showed students who scored high on N-Achievement also scored high on assertive scale.

R.S. Nair (1972) reported that N.C.C. training helps to improve significantly self-assertiveness and responsibility.

U. Pathak (1983) found that highly creative and highly intelligent students possess self-assertive tendency.

A.S. Dhaliwal (1971) conducted research on school going children and adolescents and demonstrated that Academic under achievers are generally assertive.

However S.P. Suri (1973) came to the opposite conclusion that superior students are more assertive than average and below average students.

In an experimental study by Kamalanabhans (1987) the experimental group which was subjected to an asertive study skill training showed a significant increase in achievement when compared with a control group.

While nearly in all the individual studies attempts have been made to find out which type of persons are more assertive, the foreign studies help us to know whether Assertive Training Programmes are helpful to increase assertiveness in a person.

Both type of studies together help one to have insight on the total idea of assertiveness.

K. Fischer (1976) conducted research on the effect of a verbal response model of assertiveness to develop assertiveness behaviour with the delinquents and concluded that two forms of assertive behaviour, the ability to write assertive responses and the ability to verbally formulate an assertive response in a delinquent increased as a result of assertive training programme.

K. Alyce (1976) did research on Teacher training in the use of operant principles to reinforce assertive behaviour in elementary school children. It was concluded that teachers can learn and subsequently implement operant procedures to rein-force assertive behaviour in their students. As a result of this training students were able to increase the perception of the actual frequency of their assertive behaviour. Also the ego strength of the students increase as a viable outcome of that teacher Training programme.

Alesio (1977) wanted to find out whether a short asertive training programme, to facilitate assertive behaviour has any significant effect on self-esteem and found a positive and significant correlation among the two variables.

I. Ruth (1979) did comparisons of two measures of assertiveness and the modification of non-assertive behaviours. Result
indicated that overall treatment techniques were effective in
significantly increasing the level of positive assertion from
pretest to post test.

Ingram (1980) concluded that adolescents as well as adults
can increase assertiveness and self-concept in a well organized
assertive training programme.

Rudloph (1987) made research on the effects of assertion
training on severely disabled students/clients in a residential
treatment centre. The result of the study indicated that
group assertive training may be a viable technique for increasing the severely disabled's level of assertiveness.

The data indicated that participants' scores are statistically and significantly higher on verbal measure of assertiveness than individuals who did not participate in the training
programme.

W. Thomas (1982) theme of research was "System wide implementation of an assertive discipline - based behaviour management plan - a program evaluation" The result of the study
indicated :

a)   an increase in the number of disciplinary referrals.

b)   decrease in the number of referrals due to both minor and
     severe misbehaviours.

c)   a decrease in the use of corporal punishment.

d)   an increase in the number of parent contracts.

32

J. Lockwood (1988) found that a well-organised assertive training programme was effective in the case of individual treatment with incarcerated juvenile delinquents.

Evans (1984) suggested that the groups receiving assertion training have significant higher health related self-assertion than the groups not receiving training. Increases in health related self assertion were accompanied by increase in autonomy.

K. Leonard (1982) made experimental research on personal space and the perception of assertion versus aggression. The hypotheses of his study was that a personal distance preferrence of highly assertive men would be significantly smaller than those of low assertive men. But the hypotheses did not receive statistical confirmation.

C. Stephen (1983) conducted research on the effects of demand on the cognitive assessment of assertion. The study was designed

a)   To assess the utility of multi-dimensional scaling for cognitive assertion.

b)   To assess the effects of demand on the methods of cognitive assessment.

c)   To determine whether on not all or any of these methods may be impervious to the effects of the demand.

The result of the study offered empirical support to the hypotheses.

Webb (1981) made comparison of effectiveness of group assertive training and self-esteem enhancement. The primary purpose of the study was that whether group assertive training can decreases anxiety depression and aggression and can increase self-esteem. The result indicated positive support to the Assertiveness training programme in increasing self-esteem and decreasing anxiety depression and aggression.

Ragland (1979) conducted a research of Assertive Training with juvenile delinquents. The objective of the study was to determine whether or not assertive training would a increase self-concept in a group of courat adjudged juvenile delinquents. The result indicated a positive trend toward the use of assertive behaviour.

Johnson (1979) conducted research on Assertion Training with American Indians. The result supported the hypothesis that there are cultural and racial differences in assertive response and it depends on variables such as socio-economic status and lingustic differences.

Scott (1981) conducted a research on assertion training and physically disabled subjects' effects upon locus of control. The result showed that internal locus of control and assertiveness were significantly correlated.

Leask (1981) studied the effects of Assertive Training on self-concept and locus of control of women. The result demonstrated that attitude towards occupations and assertiveness is positively related to self-concept and internal locus of control.

Boyce's (1981) theme of research was placing assertion within a situation - how other's emotional expressions influence assertive behaviour. The result showed that un-assertive subjects intention to refuse their friends' request was more dependent upon the pleasantness of their friends' reaction than the assertive subjects. Unassertive subjects experience more subjective distress in all situations. Unassertive subjects experience a more negative emotion and thought that their friends had taken the refusal more personally than did assertive subjects. The present study suggests that assertion training would benefit from focussing on the unassertive individual's reaction to other people's emotional expressions.

Canning (1982) conducted a study of the effects of group assertion training on anxiety, depression, self-concept and assertiveness in heroin addicts. Contrary to the result of other studies individuals in this investigation receiving assertion training did not significantly lower their levels of anxiety and depression.

Whlie (1986) studied the psychological investigation on the effects of cognitive and behaviour assertion training on self-efficacy. Positive relationship were found between self-efficacy and assertion training.

Hewett (1976) conducted research on interpersonal perception among college students as a function of sex and level of assertiveness and came to the conclusion that male subjects considered assertive behaviour more appropriate than female subjects. Female subjects considered assertive behaviour to a peer appropriate but assertive behaviour toward a professor inappropriate. But male subjects who were non assertive to a peer but the strongest dislike on the part of the males was directed toward other males who were non-assertive to a professor.

What emerges from all these studies that developing of assertiveness in one's behaviour is a worthwhile thing for all persons irrespective of their sex and age and in this respect assertiveness training has an important part to play whose impact is really great in the life of the individuals.

## 2.2 Sense of Responsibility :

Responsibility is the ability to fulfill one's needs. A responsible person also does that which gives him a feeling of self-worth and a feeling that he is worthwhile to others. Though it is a very important concept in the field of education there are very little evidence of research on responsibility in the Indian field of education.

M. Panda (1983) made a study on the relationship of Parental life style, Intellectual achievement, responsibility among underprivileged children and concluded that parental life style has an important part to play in enhancing the sense of responsibility among the children.

P. Roy (1982) made attempt to find out the effects of attribution training on the development of intellectual achievement responsibility and cognitive performance among lower class children and concluded that the above mentioned training has some positive effect to increase those qualities.

S. Pandey's (1983) work was on factors affecting sense of responsibility amongst higher secondary school students. Major findings of the study were that sense of responsibility was significantly higher in students belonging to the higher income group and higher academic achievement group than students belonging to lower income and achievement groups. Sense of responsibility has no significant relationship with caste, age, sex, family education, occupation and political affiliation of the family. Sense of responsibility was positively related to intelligence and level of aspiration but it was negatively related to anxiety. Sense of responsibility was predicated with the help of intellgence and level of aspiration scores. The sense of responsibility consists of two independent factors viz. psycho-social atrributes and moral attributes.

B. Rani (1980) studied self-concept and other non-cognitive factors (including responsibility) affecting the academic achievement of the scheduled caste students and found that self-concept and sense of responsibility is highly correlated.

A.S. Raghavakumari (1983) conducted a study on teacher attitudes and perceptions, affective dimensions of classroom instruction and pupil perceptions and concluded that teachers' positive perception about their students help to foster a sense of responsibility in the latter.

S. Beharawal (1987) made a study on locus of control and attribution of Responsibility for success and failure.

R.D. Singh (1985) suggested that adolescent boys and girls with a better social attitude had high responsibility.

S.P. Suri (1973) studied differential personality traits in intellectually superior, average and below average students and found that superior students have more sense of responsibility than average students.

However the foreign studies on the sense of responsibility are as follow :-

Eaves's (1978) theme of research was the effects of style focus and relevance of experience on the attribution of responsibility. The purpose of the study was to investigate the interaction effects of individual differences and environmental influences on the attribution of responsibility using an interpersonal paradiagm.

Baker (1988) studied judgements of responsibility - their relationship with self and moral reasoning in Venezuelan adolescents. The purpose of this study was to explore how adolescents understand and conduct their meaning of responsibility and to assess how these processes of understanding and constructing responsibility are related to the adolescent moral judgements and self-development.

Smith (1986) tried to compare tendencies to ascribe locus of responsibility for intellectual achievement between two groups of middle school students. The main point of the study was to investigate if statistically significant differences exist between two groups of students, those identified as emotionally impaired and those identified as regular regarding both academic success and failures. According to the study no statistically significant differences exist between two groups in terms of their locus of responsibility ascription.

Winslow (1975) suggested that self-concept of ability was significantly related to self-esteem to responsibility for academic success and responsibility for academic failure.

Forker (1978) studied social responsibility behaviour of high school senior and revealed a non-significant negative correlation between social responsibility behaviour and breadth of social concern and the importance of school as moral educator.

Crawford (1980) studied mother's attributions of causality and responsibility for achievement behaviour of their young children.

Weld (1985) made a correlational study of academic self-concept, intellectual achievement, responsibility, social cognition, and reading achievement for a sample of upper elementary school children.

Terasaw (1983) conducted a study on helplessness in learning disabled children - effects of attribution, retraining and reinforcement on personal responsibility and mathematical reasoning tasks. It was hypothesized in the study that a procedure that taught the learning disabled children to take responsibility for their behaviour would cause them to invest more effort on tasks thus leading to a change in performance. This should lead to increased persistence or increased motivation toward a task. Subsequently increased persistence should help to establish a dependent relationship between one's performance and reinforcement. Such a bond should lead to an increase in internalization of responsibility.

Clements (1991) made correlational study of awareness, sense of responsibility and commitment to learning goals. Result showed that all the variables are positively correlated with one another.

Hazel (1988) studied the effects of tutoring on reading achievement, self-concept and responsibility of 6th grade students.

McCade (1987) attempted to find out the relation between quality of school life, achievement, responsibility and creative thinking in children. Result of the study showed that more creative thinking leads to both more responsibility for achievement success and more satisfaction with structure of school.

Wylie (1985) found that academic success, feedback can affect positive academic self concept and responsibility for success in low academic self concept of students if it is presented under the proper condition.

All the above mentioned study showed that sense of responsibility is a key factor in any sphere or stage of life. Again sense of responsibility and academic achievement are highly correlated and without achieveving this sense of responsibility it is hardly possible for a student to get academic, success in school or to get success in the later period of his life.

## 2.3 Attitude toward school :

The attitude toward school refers the way the students have come to feel about their total school experience - how hard they want to work in schools, how highly they value school and how much they want to pursue further schooling. However, teacher's expectation play a definite role in students attitude toward school and performance.

Davidson and Lang (1960) found that students' perception of the teacher's feelings towards them correlated positively with their self-perception. They also found that the more positive the child's perception of his teacher's feelings, the better his academic achievement and the more desirable his classroom behaviour as rated by the teacher.

Brookover and his associates (1967) found that student's perception of the evaluation of their academic ability by teachers, parents and friends are associated with self-concept of academic ability. That is, teacher's attitudes and opinions regarding his students have a significant influence on their success in school.

Rosenthal and Jacobson (1968) demonstrated that a teacher's expectation of his pupil's intellectual functioning and competence could come to serve as an educational self-fulfilling prophency.

Sunderalakshmi (1981) compared the effects of two kinds of instructional strategy on certain student gains. The two strategies were two ways of monitoring classroom interactions. In the first strategy teacher was "initiator" and all communications during instruction were channelled through the teacher.

In the second strategy the teacher was a facilitator of interactions wherein he promoted more pupil-teacher interactions while teaching, persuaded them to work on their own and helped them in the tasks assigned.

The result showed that strategy one had greater positive influences on students' academic performance and initiative whereas strategy two had greater positive influence on classroom trust, acceptability and cohesiveness.

Kounin and Gump (1961) reported that punitive teachers in contrast to non-punitive teacher had more pupils who manifested aggression, displayed misconduct in school and cared less about learning.

Leeper (1967) concluded that pupils learn more easily and their attitude towards school improved when the teachers were friendly and respectful. Pupils' attitude toward school deteriorated when teachers were impersonal and autocratic.

Webb (1971) found that students of humanistically oriented teachers had greater morale and improved in interest as well as reported greater academic gains compared to teachers who were not sensitive to individual students.

James (1982) studied 'Reinforcement and self-concept - their relationship to attendance and attitude toward school.' The study examined the efficacy of a token contigency program in reducing school absenteeism using both a continuous and variable schedule of reinforcement. Secondly it investigated the extent to which the self-concept related to attitude toward school and overall school attendence. Result showed that absenteeism was reduced particularly among low self-concept students but there was no effect upon attitude toward school as a result of the treatment intervention.

Leonard (1989) studied the direct and indirect effect of student temperament on school achievement and attitude toward school. The result indicated that students who are most likely to succeed in school are those who evoke high teacher expectations and perceive their class room experiences in a positive light.

Ingram (1976) conducted study on "a study of student attitude toward school." The study suggested that it is possible to administer a survey instrument to locate not only critical deviations in student attitude toward school in given school system but also to identify early indications of the detrioration of positive attitudes at various levels. While the attitude of boys and girls toward various aspects of the school environment^have^ similar tendencies, the overall attitude of girls was significantly more positive than that of the boys.

Ruth (1984) conducted research on 'an examination of the relationship among students' self-concept, level of anxiety and attitude toward school. The findings of the study appear to indicate a statistically significant relationship among the variables.

Herriolt (1986) made a study entitled "a study of the self-concept and attitude toward school of gifted and general students and of teacher attitude toward these students". Result indicated that formal identification of academically gifted students and the provision of special programme for the student resulted in significantly more positive self-concept in intellectual and school status and significantly more positive attitude toward school. Teachers also indicated a generally more positive attitude toward them.

Herriolt (1986) made a study entitled "a study of the self-concept and attitude toward school of gifted and general students and of teacher attitude toward these students". Results indicated that formal identification of academically gifted students and the provision of special programme for the students resulted in significantly more positive self-concept in intellectual and school status and significantly more positive attitude toward school. Teachers also indicated a generally more positive attitude toward them.

Graves (1980) tried to find out how school achievement and attitude toward school are influenced by a set of demographic, ecological & psychological variables. Findings showed that achievement orientation emerged as a strong predictor of both school grades and attitude toward school. School enrollment size influences attitude toward school, primarily through perceived crowding.

MacDonald's (1981) study was on 'Thai vocational school students' self-esteem, alienation and attitude toward school. Result showed that Thai vocational high school students when compared with students from academic schools had lower self-esteem scores, they felt more alienated from their society, they felt more negatively toward their school.

Platt's (1985) work was on the relationship of self-concept social comparison process, study habits and attitude toward school in private and public school. Empirical result focused on the significant positive relationship among the variables.

Reimer (1977) wanted to see how a humanistic interaction treatment programme could help students to have positive attitude toward school and their teachers. The result of the study supported the contention that humanistic educational programme is very helpful to bring the above mentioned change in students.

Gordon's (1979) work was on "the effects of teachers' verbal/nonverbal behaviour upon students' attitude toward school, teacher and self". The study indicated no significant difference in students' attitude toward school teacher or self which was related to teacher's verbal/nonverbal behaviour. But

44

when grade level was considered the findings indicated that grade
level influence students' attitude toward school.

Shearn (1979) worked on 'an analysis of self-concent and
attitude toward school, between emotionally disturbed and normal
school aged children. The result of this investigation concluded that emotionally disturbed group and a group of normal
children matched for sex, age, intelligence and urban background were more similar in self-concept and attitude toward
school than dissimilar.

Denzin (1978) tried to find out children's perception of
mother-teacher similarity and attitude toward school. The
conclusion reached were that there is a significant relationship
between attitude toward school and children's perception of
mother-teacher similarity in the population studied.

Brandon (1979) worked on the relationship of density and
sex to self-concept and the cognitive and effective components
of black high school students' attitude toward school.

V. Chaturvedi (1981) studied achievement and attitudes of
students to school in relation to direct and indirect behaviour
of teacher in the classroom.

B. Kour's (1984) work was on 'a study of attitude toward
school of IX grade boys and girls in relation to achievement
motivation.

R. Kulshrestha (1983) tried to find out the interrelation
among value orientation, interests and attitudes school as
correlates of self-concept of male and female adolescents.

V.R. Rawal's (1985) theme of research was 'Personality adjustment and attitude toward school of emotionally disturbed adolescent in relation to their home and school environment.

John & Abraham (1981) found that high achievers had a positive attitude toward teachers, school and academic work.

Nirmal Kumari (1979) made a study on 'Personality, Intelligence, Achievement Motivation, Attitude toward school and study methods as predictors of Academic Achievement.

Vijayalakshmi's (1983) study was on school achievement and students' attitude toward school as related to some demographic and psychological variables.

V.B. Chauhan (1981) made a comparative study on life tendencies, meaning of success, self-concept and attitude toward school among Harijan and Non-Harijan students.

V.S. Waghaye (1983) also made a comparative study of attitudes of scheduled castes and scheduled tribe pupils toward school and teachers.

S.K. Saxena (1981) tried to find out the relation of self-concept, study habits and attitude toward school as correlates of socio-economic status and cultural setting in different divisions of High School students of Kanpur district.

Sukhchand (1977) found that the reading achievement of disadvantaged students in grades VII, VIII and IX was related to their attitude toward school and the better rewards tended to have better attitude toward school than did the poorer readers.

Tiwari (1979) found a significant relationship between student's attitude toward the school and school achievement.

Rao (1966) found among the students of standard VIII in Delhi that intelligence, study habit, and school attitude were significantly related to the prediction of scholastic achievement.

Chopra (1982) also found that secondary school students attitude toward education had a very high positive correlation with academic achievement.

Bhaduri (1971) and Saxena (1972) found that the over-achievers had a positive attitude toward school, study and school work. Whereas Srivastava (1967) found that no significant relationship existed between under achievement and attitude toward school.

Zacharia (1977) found among the secondary school pupils in Kerala that there was high positive correlation between pupil achievement in social studies and their attitude toward social studies.

Jain (1979) found among the high school students of Jammu that attitude toward mathematics was one of the factors that played a vital role in learning mathematics.

Sarah (1983) reported that the attitude of high school students towards science and science education in Tamil Nadu was generally favourable but there was a wide disparity in their attitude toward school.

From all the above mentioned studies it is clear that positive attitude toward school is a very important factor getting academic success in school. Therefore parents as well as teachers should try their utmost to foster this quality among students.

## 2.4 Educational Aspiration :

There are varieties of researches on Educational Aspiration undertaken in India as well as in foreign countries.

However Rosenfeld and Zander (1961) define aspiration as the level of achievement realistically expected by an individual. In another study Rosenfeld (1964) equates level of aspiration with the difficulty level of the goal selected by a person.

According to Burnard (1972) the term level of aspiration refers to the level of performance to which one aspires in the future because of his success or failure in preceeding tasks. It is closely related to the concept which an individual has about himself and his powers. Edward and Seannell's (1968) view of level of aspiration as something that pertains to goal setting and goal achievement and Eysenck (1970) treated level of aspiration as a personality trait.

Emmit and Albert (1965) in their study pointed three generalized variables as being of major importance in structuring the aspiration of high school youths - the knowledge held by the youth with regard to the various occupational roles, the manners in which the various occupational alternatives were evaluated by him and the self-evaluation by the student in which he assessed the likelihood of successful performance in the various roles.

Karl and Edward (1976) found that academic ability and status origin as important determinant of educational aspiration.

Berger and Chey (1975) in a longitudinal study investigated the correlation between educational aspiration and educational achievement. Several correlational studies have found strong relationship among children's self-concept educational aspiration and their educational achievement. (Bledsoe 1967, Brookover, Thomas & Patterson 1964, Epps 1969, Rosenberg and Simons 1973, Walterberg and Clifford 1964, Goswami 1978 ) All of these studies reported that the positive self-concept of school ability is significantly related to educational aspiration.

Kausler (1959) and Ali (1969) established a significant positive relationship between educational aspiration and academic performance.

Harrill (1962) found significant difference in the level of aspiration of high and low achievers.

Ferrone (1984) conducted a study - the primary concept of which was to provide the educators with an insight into educational aspiration and expectations of high school students, related to students' perceived parental encouragement, achievement and locus of control. Result indicated significant relationship among the variables.

In India Ramkumar and Vasantha (1972) found that adequate appraisal of one's aspiration can be conducive to improve achievement to the level to which one's intelligence will permit.

Umiyal and Shukla (1973) from their study 'Academic achievement and behaviour in the level of aspiration situation' had come to the conclusion that educational aspiration vis a vis academic achievement is significantly and positively related with flexibility and performance score.

Pandey et al (1975) in their experimental study had found that increased level of aspiration resulted in a significant increase in academic achievement.

Shah et al (1971) found a strong relationship between the educational aspiration and academic achievement of post high school students.

Arap Rono (1982) attempted to identify the characteristic related to expressed educational and occupational aspiration and expectations of secondary school students.

Menon (1972) found that job aspiration and educational aspiration were strongly associated with high achievement particularly for girls.

Phutela's (1976) study in the states of Haryana and Punjab identified educational and vocational aspiration as specific predictors of academic achievement for the total sample.

Whereas Hussain's (1977) study found that students with low aspirations showed unrealistic and defensive attitude resulting in low achievement.

On the contrary Sharma (1979) found that the level of aspiration did not influence the academic achievement of high school and intermediate students.

Chopra (1982) found that significantly large number of first class students belonged to higher socio-eco status and they had higher educational and occupational aspirations.

Gupta (1981) reported that level of aspiration correlated negatively and significantly with academic achievement for the total sample and also to high socio-economic arts boys and science girls.

Jasuja (1983) found that the level of aspiration and frustration did affect the achievement.

Das (1986) found educational aspiration as the second powerful predictor of academic achievement.

Adiseshia and Ramanathan (1974) Dubey (1974) Pimpley (1974) and Sachidananda (1974) found that scheduled caste and scheduled tribe students had high educational aspiration.

But Gangrade (1974) reported low educational aspirations among scheduled caste students.

Koul (1983) found a low level of aspiration among the tribal failure students at middle and matriculation level.

Pandey (1985) found that the low deprived students scored significantly higher than high deprived students' on level of aspiration.

Therefore educational aspiration is the educational level which an individual wishes to reach. Its role is very important in the field of education as an individual's achievement can't be viewed as successful or unsuccessful unless a statement of his level of aspiration is obtained.

## 2.5  Academic Achievement :

Academic Achievement is the measuring rod to serve the purpose of evaluation in education. Academic Achievement is a 'sine qua non' in the school context. School as a functionery of formal education tends to emphasize achievement which facilitates the process of role allocation for the social system. However, in this study by Academic Achievement it is meant how well the students are doing in their subjects of study as are required by the school syllabus and how the students' sense of achievement regarding academics is increasing.

Ample evidences exist of relationship between intelligence and academic achievement. Eysenck (1947) reviewed 600 titles and concluded that the correlation between intelligence and achievement varies between 0.50 to 0.60 while Froehlich & Hoyt (1959) found the range between 0.30 to 0.80 in their review of 10.3 studies.

A vast number of studies by Jordan (1923),Thurstone (1925) Edds & McCall (1933),Burt (1939), Cohler (1941), Vermat et al (1966),Sudame (1973), Rastogi (1974), Seetha (1975), Ameerjan, Girija and Bhadra (1978) and many others have found positive relationship between intelligence & academic achievement. In the area of socio-economic status Dave & Dave (1971), Menon 1973) , Abraham (1974), Dewal (1974), Chandra (1975), Halloway (1980), Khan (1980), Bolgiani (1984) etc. established significant positive relationship between socio-eco status and academic achievement.

The relationship between peergroup influence and academic achievement had also been evaluated by some other studies e.g. Cocalis (1972), Golden (1972), Badami & Badami (1975), Howton (1979).

Different socio-psychological factors concerned with the
student tend to occupy a pertinent place in that measurement
process. Basically education is a social process a group
related activity. Therefore it is necessary to find out the
proper placement of group related factors along with its
relative impact on academic achievement.

Dave (1963) and Wolf (1964) examined relations between the
family environment and measure   of academic achievement and
intelligence respectively. Wolf identified three press variables
in the home environment, which he postulated as being related to
intelligence. There were press for achievement motivation,
press for language development and provisions for general
learning.

In Dave's study six press variables defined the family
environment, achievement press language models, academic
guidance, activeness of the family, intellectuality in the home
and work habits in the family. The result indicated that the
press variables have differential relations with performance
in the academic sybjects. For example  the environment accounts
for our 50% of the variance in arithmetic problem solving,
reading and word knowledge, but only 31% of the variance in
arithmetic computation scores. Also the order of importance
of the predictability of the six press variables was found to
differ from subject to subject. In the case of word knowledge
and reading achievement press was the most important variable
in a step wise regression analysis, while for arithmetic problem
solving the most important variable was intellectuality in the
home.

Laosa (1982) sought to study a combination of process and status variables operating in the home environment. This causal model hypothesized an inter-relationship between the background variables like the mother's education, the mother's occupation amount of reading she does mediated by variables like mother's socio-educational values, the maternal modeling also considered were child's age, child's sex and amount of reading done with the child by family members other than the parents. The findings revealed the positive influence of maternal modeling on child's intellectual development. /

Marjoribanks (1973) examined relations between the family environment and scores on tests of verbal, numerical, spatial and reasoning ability. Marjoribank's study emphasizes the importance of father involvement in the son's activities.

Bing (1963) found that mothers of high verbal boys (boys who had high verbal scores in relation to their number and spatial scores) in comparison to mothers of low verbal boys provided more stimulation in early childhood, were more critical of poor academic achievement, provided more story books and let boys take greater part in meal time conversations.

Results of Honzik (1967) Bing (1963) and other studies by Ferguson and Maccoby (1966) showed that in general our involvement with parents may impede the relative development of divergent number ability, while it is fostered in homes which allow boys a considerable degree of uninterrupted free time and freedom to experiment on their own.

The family environment studies have been conducted in diverse setting on varied age groups. A few of such studies Fraser (1958), Wiseman (1967), Plowden (1967) report that the

family environment measures account for more of the variance in
the achievement scores than in the intelligence test scores.
Further environment accounted for a large percent of variance
for the aspiration scores of the children but is unable to
effectively account for the other personality and affective
variables.

The main conclusion from all these studies was that the
school can't successfully remediate a child from a home that
does not provide the basic and that the best home cannot fully
take the place of the school.

Cannellas (1979) attempt with 112 first grade students
proved that the group seriation and mental imagery subtests
made significant positive contributions to the multiple corre-
lations with each of the achievement areas, arithmetic, reading and language. The variance in achievement explained by the
various combination of group cognitive tasks were 13% in reading 20% in language and 33% in arithmetic.

Taloumis (1979) through his research found that scores on
conservation tasks could be used as predictors of academic achievement from first through third grades. Canter (1975) who worked
with the Kindergarten children and followed them through the
third grade found that conservation was significant predictor
of achievement at the Kindergarten and first grade levels.

Omotoso (1975) also found that there existed a strong
relationship between mathematics achievement and conservation
seriation and classification abilities.

Jain (1965) sought to investigate into the relationship between home environment and scholastic achievement. The study revealed that the influence of home environment on achievement was found to be positive and significant and that the influence of intelligence on school achievement was found to be the greatest and that it had higher relationship with achievement of boys as compared to that of girls.

Barial (1966) attempted to explore the relationship between the social class background, achievement motivation and achievement of class tenth students. The investigation revealed that there existed no significant difference in the educational achievement, achievement motivation and intelligence of students belonging to various social classes.

Studies by Chopra (1964) and Chopra (1982) explored the relationship between certain socio-economic factors and achievement. The findings revealed that children whose fathers were professionals were certain of continuing their education while majority of children whose father were skilled and unskilled laborers were uncertain of their future education (Chopra 1964).

Anand (1973) found that socio-economic environment influences the mental abilities and academic achievement.

Sutradhar (1982) in his research attempted to enquire into the relative academic achievement of the socially advantaged and disadvantaged children and to find out the socio-psychological factors associated with their relative academic achievement. The major findings showed although they do not differ in respect to intelligence the advantaged children were always superior to the disadvantaged children

in respect to their academic achievement. The advantaged
families were characterized with more child centeredness and
positive self concept of the father and the child, the reverse
was found to be true for the disadvantaged group. The academic
achievement for both the groups had significant association with
the environment and biographic factors.

A research attempt by Chatterji Mukherjee and Banerjee
(1971) sought to investigate into the effect of some important
aspects of social class such as income, parents education, family
size, general condition of home etc. upon the scholastic achievement. Interestingly they found that the economic conditions of
the family seemed to have no effect upon the scholastic achievement in all the intellectual ability groups. Similarly posse-
ssion of a study room had no favourable effect in increasing
the achievement score in almost all the cases. The other
aspects showed that the family size and the number of sibling
were inversely related to the scholastic achievement specially
in the low intellectual level. In some cases parents help had
significant positive contribution towards higher achievement,
parents educational level was directly related to the achievement of their children, however father's occupation was not
found to be consistently related to children's achievement.

Srinivasa Rao and Subrahmanyan (1982) sought to study the
factors influencing the reading attainment of primary school
children. The findings were home condition, school conditions
and personal attributes of children collectively affect the
academic achievement.

Another approach in studying the factors what differentiates
the over and under achivers, specifically in terms of their
background variables. Such research attempts exploring into

the causes of academic over and under achievement have come out with consistent findings in these respective studies (Mathur, 1963), Srivastava(1967),Menon(1973), Tandon (1978), Dave & Dave (1971), Agarwal (1975), Chaudhuri and Jain (1975).

The findings of these studies showed that  -

It was found that the high achievers usually had parents with higher level of education specially mothers (Chaudhari & Jain, 1975).

Parents of overachievers gave more importance to education and provided their children with the required guidance.

Apart from the above mentioned general findings these studies also showed some more pertinent observations.

Srivastava (1967) found that among other factors under achievement was related to problems concerning the family and to background and personal factors like age, socio-economic status, father's profession,size of family, number of siblings, birth order, reading interests, failure in school examination and participation in games and sports.

Tandon (1978) showed that the physical, emotional  and socio-economic conditions of the male group of under achievers were not whole some.  Their parents were academically less qualified had professions which were less remunerative and had large families.  However the home environment was not found to be a relevant factor in under achievement of female under-achievements.

Dave and Dave (1971) concluded that the non-verbal intelligence of the rank students was superior to that of failed students, next there existed significant differences in the intelligence of students coming from homes having differential parental income and occupations. It was also found that the higher percentage of failed students belonged to homes having lower parental income, education and occupation. Also like in other research findings parents of rank students showed more academic concern about their ward than those of failed students.

From the above mentioned studies it appear that there is a positive relation between intelligence and achievement. Academic achievement is also positively related with home environment, intellectuality in the home parents educational level, and occupation, child's age, sex etc. However, the economic condition of the family seemed to have no effect upon the scholastic achievement. On the other hand underachievement was related to problem concerning the background of the family and personal factors like socio-economic status, father's profession, size of family, number of sibling, birth order, reading interests, failure in school examination & participation in games and sports.

## 2.6 Self-concept :

Self-concept is the way people describe themselves based on the roles they play and the personal attributes they think they possess. Rogers (1959) defined self-concept as the organized consistent conceptual gestalt composed of perceptions of the relationship of the I or me to others and to various aspects of life together with the values attached to those perceptions.

Ramkumar (1969) has defined self-concept as cluster of most personal meaning a person attributes to himself.

According to Saroja (1991) self-esteem is formed when individual perceive themselves as capable worthy and accept themselves. Development of positive self-concept is the basis for the development of self-esteem.

Purkey (1970) explained that a person has countless beliefs about himself, not all equally significant. It includes only those perceptions about himself which seem most vital or important. Purkey further explained that the maintenance and enhancement of perceived self is the motive behind all our activities. We evaluate the world and its meaning in terms of how we see ourselves.

It is generally accepted that schools ought to and do develop learning in a variety of areas, including personal and social development. In fact, intrinsic to the notion of the hidden curriculum is the idea that the self and social outcomes of schooling are powerful equals if not more powerful than academic outcomes.

A persistent relationship has been found between various aspects of self-perceptions and a wide variety of school related variables which have been found to be related to self-concept are school achievement, perceived social status among peers, participation in class discussion, completion of school, perceptions of peers and teachers, pro-social behaviour and self-direction in learning. Students carry images of the self in several areas as well as the potential for developing many more. These might include the self as person, as learner, as academic achiever, as peer and others. Each experience in school can affect self-concept personally held values and/or the subsequent self-esteem of the learner. For this reason an understanding of self-concept and esteem in general, how they function in youth and how the schools might enhance or hinder them must be a major concern of those responsible for curriculum planning and implementation.

Deibert and Hoy (1977) found that students in humanistic school demonstrated higher degree of self-actualization than those in school with a custodial orientation. This correlational research has obvious implications for schools when one examines the qualities associated with each type of climate. The custody climate is characterized by concern for maintenance of order, preference for autsocratic procedures, student stereotyping, punitive sanctions and impersonalness. The humanistic climate is characterized by democratic procedures, student participation in decision making, respect, self-discipline, interaction and flexibility. In other words it appears that the custodial climate may be a debilitating factor in the concept of self while the humanistic climate might be considered facilitating (Licata and Wildes 1980, Estep, Willower and Licata 1982).

Both Campbell (1956) and Bledsoe (1967) using self-report inventories found a stronger relationship between the self-concept and achievement in boys than in girls. In 1960 Shaw Edson and Bell conducted a study to determine differences between achievers and under achievers perceptions of themselves. A major conclusion of the study was that male achievers felt relatively more positive about themselves than male underachievers.

Gill found patterns of achievement significantly related
to the perceived self in public school students.

Cole (1968) explored the relationship between the reported
self-concepts and school adjustment of 80 sixth grade students
and found significant positive correlation between their self-
concepts and such variables as reading and mathematical achievement.

Farquhar's (1968) study showed that over and under achievers
responded with significant differences to items designed to
measure their reflected self-concept and that students with high
academic productivity tended to have high self-concepts. In an
extensive research project Brookover and his associates completed three projects (1962 to 1968). Among their findings were
that reported self-concept of ability is significantly related
to achievement among both boys and girls. But this study led
Brookover to hypothesize that confidence in one's academic is a
necessary but not sufficient factor in determining scholastic
success. The findings that socially disabled students do not
necessarily report low self-concepts is borne out by a study by
Soares and Soares (1969) who completed a comparative study of the
self-perceptions of disadvantaged and advantaged elementary
school children and found on the whole more positive self-
perceptions among the disadvantaged than the advantaged
children. A composit portrait of the successful student would
seem to show that he has a relatively high opinion of himself
and is optimistic about his future performance (Ringness 1961).
He has confidence in his general ability (Taylor 1964) and in
his ability as a student (Brookover 1969). He needs fewer
favourable evaluation from others (Dittes 1959) and he feels
that he works hard is liked by other students and is generally
polite and honest (Davidson and Greenberg 1967). Studies which
support the notion that underachievers tend to have negative

self-concepts are numerous. In 1960 Goldberg studied underachievers and found that the underachievers was found to
perceive himself as less able to fulfill required tasks, less
eager to learn, less confident and less ambitious. In 1961
Show reported that underachievers have a more negative self-
concept than achievers and demonstrate less mature behaviour
than achieving peers. Bruck & Bodwin (1962) found a positive
relationship between educational disability and immature self-
concept. In 1963 Show and Alves attempted to verify previous
findings and reported that male achievers and underachievers
reported significant difference on the variables on self-
concept, self-acceptance and the self-acceptance of peers.

Combs (1963) studied the relationship between self-
perception and underachievement in high school boys and found
that underachievers see themselves as less adequate and less
acceptable to others and that they find their peers and adults
less acceptable.

Taylor's (1964) finding was that underachievers have feeling of inadequacy, have a depressed attitude toward themselves
and have strong inferiority feelings.

However, Holland (1959) found that the underachievers tend
to have positive self-concept. But judging by the preponderance
of available researches it seems reasonable to assume that
unsuccessful students are likely to hold attitudes about themselves and their abilities which are pervasively negative. They
tend to see themselves as less able less, adequate and less
self-reliant than their more successful peers.

In India also there were several studies on self-concept
P.Deao (1967) conducted a study on self-concept of disciplined
students. S.K. Bhalla (1970) also made a comparative study of
the self-concepts of disciplined and indisciplined students.
The result suggested that the indisciplined groups describe
themselves through greater number of a adjectives, perceiving
themselves as graceful, likeable, amiable, energetic forceful
etc. whereas the other groups perceive themselves to be shy
introvert, socially withdrawn, patient, well adjusted and relaxed.
Both the groups consider themselves to be kind, cooperative,
friendly, self-controlled etc. Both the groups differ significantly on emotional adjustment and social adjustment. The
mean score on self-concept of indisciplined students are lower
than that of the disciplined students.

The objective of the study of Goswami (1978) was to study
the self-concept of the school going adolescents and its
relationship to sex, intelligence, scholastic achievement and
adjustment. The findings of the study showed that the global
self-concept of male adolescent were significantly different
from that of female adolescents. Self-concept and intelligence
had a significant positive correlation. Self-concept mean score
of urban and rural students had no significant difference,
global self-concept and scholastic achievement had a significant positive correlation and self-concept and adjustment had
a significant positive correlation.

Ramkumar (1969) aimed at studying the relationship between
the self-concept and achievement of college students and the
influence of certain variables on that relationship. Findings
showed that positive relationship existed between self-concept
and achievement, between self-concept and intelligence. The
intelligence and achievement of high and low achievers could
be differentiated on their self-concept scores.

Sumitra Patel (1973) in her study titled 'An investigation
to study self-esteem changes as function of counselling Therapy'
tried to enhance self-esteem using group counselling. Her
approach to counselling was based on Roger's client centered
Therapy. The results showed that the low self-esteem and high
self-esteem subjects both showed changes in the level of their
self-esteem under the influence$_\wedge$counselling interviews.
                                      of

Choksi (1976) conducted an experiment using Psychological
education input in primary school children of Baroda city and
and studied its effectiveness on academic performance as well
as traits like motivation, adjustment, anxiety, class-room
trust and self-image. Her finding showed a significant positive gain in pupil's adjustment trust and self-image.

Laxmi (1976) developed an input programme for teacher
trainees of training college and found its effect on self-
perception. The study revealed that there was significant
difference in self-scale. The programme developed positive
attitude towards self, optimism and respect for self. It also
resulted in improving self-confidence and self-perception of
teacher trainees.

Olivia (1985) developed educational input for the enhancement of self-concept and achievement motivation in the
first year degree students of Apostolic Carmel Colleges. The
study demonstrated that her psychological education input
programme was effective in increasing self concept and
N-achievement of college students.

Thomas (1987) and Saroja (1991) developed input programmes
for teachers and students to orient the experimental class
along a humanistic orientation characterized by caring and

positive relationship between teachers and the students and among the students themselves. The study has shown growth in some psychological dimension like self-concept, inter-personal relation, cooperation and academic achievement.

From the review of the above studies it is confirmed that, self-concept plays a crucially important role and that it can be enhanced by people, programmes and policies (Purkey 1970). The source of all our behaviour including learning is the concept that we have about ourselves. As our behaviour emerges from our self concept and tends to maintain it, changing self concept is the most crucial task to achieve.

2.7. Researches on Reality Therapy :

Various works both theoretical and experimental have been conducted on Reality Therapy. There are numerous researches on Reality Therapy, nearly on every aspect of human life. Here the investigator has chosen only those important works which have relevance with the present study.

However, the works on application of Reality Therapy on other aspects of human life have been added in the appendix to show the versatile applicability of the therapy.

Renna ( 1984) in "The use of control theory and Reality Therapy with students who are out of control" described effective Reality Therapy techniques in crisis intervention for teachers and counselors working with out-of-control (OOC) students and clients. The Keystone of the technique lay in the ability of the students to make value judgements that their behaviour was not helping and then to make a commitment to change. Redirectional techniques called "Cognitive hooks" helped the OOC persons to use the thinking component of their

66

total behaviour to gain control. The steps involved exploring
the picture or perception of what happened, reframing or
changing the way students thought and felt about the problem
and the therapy helped students to take responsibility for
their behaviour, self-evaluation planning and commitment to
change.

Fried (1984) in "Reality and Self control - discussed
William Glasser's description of behaviour as the attempt to
reduce the difference between desires and reality in the
context of 'out of control' students. *Procedures* described by
Glasser (1986) were presented to help student personnel workers
to rebuild a trusting human relationship with students. The
procedures included -

1.   Becoming friends with students.
2.   Helping students analyze their own behaviour in detail.
3.   Teaching students to identify and set priorities and
4.   Being unwilling to accept excuses.

Pearl (1986) in "Increasing the appropriate behaviour of
two third grade students with Reality Therapy - A pilot study"
conducted a pilot study to determine whether reality therapy
could increase the frequency of appropriate behaviour and
enhance the interaction of students with peers and the classroom teachers. A 9 year old male and a 8 year old female with
behavioural difficulties in a 3rd grade mainstream classroom
were the students. An observational instrument was developed
which evaluated on task/off task behaviour and positive or
negative interactions between.

(a)   Students and students.
(b)   Students and teachers.

Over a 6 week period students were observed during a
baseline and a treatment phase with Reality Therapy. Samples
of behaviour were collected and were analyzed by a percentage
agreement statistics. It is concluded that the successful use
of Reality Therapy technique facilitated a positive change in
behaviour in both the students.

Butzin (1990) in "School discipline - A new management
system that works" presented a four phase positive discipline
plan based on William Glasser's Reality Therapy. The goal of
the plan was to teach the students to assume responsibility
for their own action. Discipline was instructional as opposed
to punitive. A record was kept for each child upon which all
serious behaviour instructions were written.

During phase 1, the teacher dealt with the students
directly, evaluated possible cause of inappropriate behaviour
and attempted to find and reward positive aspects of the
student behaviour. After three infractions, the student met
with the teacher and developed a written plan to change the
behaviour. The parents were informed about the problem and
the students plan for change. If there were continuing
behaviour problems ( 6-10 infractions phase-2 ) the student
met with the principal and school counselor and developed
another written plan for changing behaviour.

Ten or more infraction (Phase-3) called for a meeting of
the student with the teacher, principal, counselor and parents
and the development of another written plan for behavioural
change. Misbehaviour beyond that point (Phase-4) resulted in
suspension and work with a behaviour specialist.

Sarah (1982) in "School Discipline programmes that work"
had successfully operated a Time out/Discipline Model program
in their middle school for five years. The program was
developed from 1978-1981. Two major goals had proven statistically successful.

(1) Students chose responsible behaviour and reduced the
    number of times they were sent out of the classroom for
    inappropriate behaviour and

(2) Classroom teachers and the principal increased instruct-
    ional time and decreased time spent on discipline.

The program was based upon Reality Therapy. The concepts
of Reality Therapy included involvement with the students as a
caring friend, concern with present behaviour not past behaviour
students' acknowledgement of the appropriateness of the chosen
behaviour, development of a plan for better behaviour which
included referral to the time out room for help, student
commitment to the plan, no excuses if the commitment was
broken and no punishment but rather fair and consistent
consequences for choosing unacceptable behaviour. Two components
were proved essential for the success of the program.

    (a) entire staff commitment and
    (b) a full time person available in the Time out area.

Young (1973) in "Discipline with a purpose" discussed
classroom discipline in the light of the ideas of R.Dreikurs
(1971) and William Glasser (1969). Logical discipline taught
students that they were responsible for their behaviour and
that every behaviour provided a benefit or a penalty to the
student. Teachers refused to accept excuses for failures,
communicated to students that they were capable and worthwhile.

Richard (1977) in "Implementing an Inservice programm in positive discipline strategies provided positive discipline strategies to Kentucky Junior high school students based on William Glasser's Reality Therapy over a period of two years (1974-1976). Four program elements were emphasized to ensure the teachers' and administrators' sense of commitment to and ownership of the program.

(1) Collaborative decision making among teachers, students and administrator.

(2) Long term training and support by university personnel with a full time trainer at the school for the first year.

(3) Identification of existing practices and the contigurations of changes to be implemented in school rules, teacher disciplinary actions, Administrator actions and

(4) The evaluation of data measuring the stages of concern and the level of use of the innovation.

The importance of teachers' and administrators' commitment to a new program was noted. As shown by the decline in student suspension, expulsion and days lost, the program was succesully imolemented.

Rudner (1987) in "A practical model for controlling a group of off behaviour problem children in the classroom" described a model combining a behavioural approach with Reality Therapy which was used to control a group of behaviour problems in the classroom. A behaviour modification design to the token economy system was established together with a classroom atmosphere of Warmth and understanding. The children

were helped to recognize what they were doing and their responsibility for it. In this design the children earned and/or
lost certain rewards depending on their daily classroom
behaviour. Difficulties that may arise and suggested, solutions to these are discussed.

Crow (1979) in "Social agency practice based on Reality
Therapy/control theory" described the work of a foster care
agency that used Reality Therapy in the treatment of children
and teenagers with special problems. Learning to function as
a successful member in a foster home was the basic treatment
for the client. Training was given to staff client and foster
parents in Reality Therapy and control theory. An interview
study of the staff foster parents and clients associated with
the agencys office indicated extensive and effective use of
the concepts and techniques of Reality Therapy and control
theory to teach clients to satisfy wants by exhibiting
responsible behaviours.

Epstein (1989) in "Treating delinquent prone adolescents
and preadolescents" described an after school treatment
programme that provided academic remediation and socialization
for preadolescents and adolescents males with a history of as
acting out at home, in school and in the community. The treatment methodology of the program bore a close resemblance to
Reality Therapy with its focus on the general refusal to accept
past history as an unrelenting determinant or execuse for
current behaviour. The program consisted of a sequence of
activities that provided recreation guided socialization,
experiences academic remediation and group therapy.

Watkins (1990) in "Combining the child discipline approaches to Alfred Adler and William Glasser - A case study" presented the case of 12 year old male with behaviour problems to illustrate how the disciplinary approaches of Alfred Adler (1956) and William Glasser (1965) were used to effect changes in the students' behaviour. A treatment plan addressed three areas -

i)  The therapeutic relationships.
ii)  The classroom intervention.
iii)  Family intervention.

Following treatment, students demonstrated little misbehaviour and assumed a more responsible role at home.

Page (1991) in "The effects of a program of behaviour modification and Reality Therapy on the behaviour of Emotionally disturbed Institutionalized Adolescent" used behaviour modification and Reality Therapy to bring positive behaviour changes in twenty severly retarded emotionally disturbed adolescents as measured on two adaptive behaviour scales.

Smith (1980) in "Serving troubled youth - quality programmes" presented three approaches to the problems of troubled and disturbed youth and described group therapeutic discussion based on William Glasser's Reality Therapy in which students earned points for responsible behaviour and task completion and an integrated approach to drug and alcohol.

Brown (1983) in "The effects of individual cotracting and guided group interaction upon behaviour disordered youth's self-concept" determined the effect on self-concept of guided group interaction on 25 male and 5 female of 13-18 years old

who had been referred to a youth centre by a juvenile court,
school, or parents contracted goals centered around cognitive
of psychomotor domains. Emphasis in the group interaction was
on Glassers Reality Therapy. Preparation of self was measured
by F.M. Bower and N.M. Lambert's self-test scale which uses 40
items to determine degree of congruence between perceived and
ideal self comparison of preprogram with postprogram scores
show that the individual's ideal self perception changed
following the intervention while there was no significant
change in real self score with the result that real and ideal
self perception were closer after intervention than before.
Results tend to indicate that the program promoted a more
realistic and mature self-orientation.

Kruger (1985) in "A child care treatment plan for the self-
development of emotionally disturbed children" described a
treatment plan for institutionalized emotionally disturbed boys
designed and implemented by a team of child care workers.
Teaching of skills needed for life in society was emphasised
through the guidelines of Reality Therapy. Each child received
an individual treatment program and daily records of progress
were kept. The treatment aimed at self-improvement through a
feeling of self worth. Two basic steps of the programme were:

(a)   increase self-confidence through group participation.
(b)   cooperation with others toward a common goal.

Bratter (1987) in "Treating alienated unmotivated drug
abusing adolescents" considered that a reality - therapy based
psychotherpeutic approach was effective in treating alienated
unmotivated drug abusing adolescents. Once the adolescent boy
was confronted with his self-destructive behaviour, the
counselor must become advocate, suporter, champion and representative, thus forcing behaviour change through direct intervention.

Meyer (1993) in "Birth and life of an incentive system in a residential institution for adolescents" described the development of an incentive system based on William Glasser's Reality Therapy for use in residential institution for adolescent adjusted, neglected and dependent. The system involved assignment in an ascending order of expected mastery of problems and increasing privileges.

Gramstad (1991) in "The application of Reality Therapy in a problem-driver program" discussed how Reality Therapy concepts were applied in shaping the content of an educational course for problem drivers. Early in the class, participants addressed issues dealing with thinking, feeling right or wrong behaviour and the perceived fairness of receiving a citation. In later segments participants identified personal needs and wants and developmental picture albums through group activities Materials included an inventory designed to elicit a driver needs profile and a video-tap displaying effective ineffective and 'band aid' behaviour. After viewing the video-tap, participants identified alternative behaviours selected effective behaviours and developed plans to carry out those behaviours.

Cohen (1977) in "Using Reality Therapy with adult offenders" presented a modified version of Reality Therapy as understood and applied in work with adult offenders in a variety of practice settings. Reality Therapy seeked to enable the client to attain an innate sense of personal responsibility and to gain conscious mastery of his/her behaviour. The practice theory as developed here was rooted in the writings of William Glasser (1964, 1965). The normative principles underlying the theory were discussed and the 5 basic treatment techniques - involvement, current behaviour, evaluation of behaviour, planning, commitment are outlined and illustrated via case vigneltes. It was concluded that Reality Therapy could provide a path to more responsible behaviour for most adult offenders.

Williams (1980) in "Reality Therapy in a correctional institution" presented that 43 male adolescents inmates participated in a 15 week pilot program in Reality Therapy (RT) which stressed the active role the client must take to change his style of living. Five groups engaged in three successive five week contract, negotiated between inmates and therapist. Each contract required a greater behavioural effort on the part of the inmate than the previous one. Inmates anonmously completed a questionnaire at the end of the program. Only 18 had participated in any previous group program and these voted overwhelmingly (16 to 2) that Reality Therapy was better than the previous program. Over 80% rated the program as being very helpful to them and almost 80% enjoyed it very much. Participants liked Reality Therapy because it gave them the opportunity to find out more about themselves and become more responsible to deal with reality and it helped them to have responsible outlook on life in genral and prison in particular No inmate received a disciplinary report during the program's 15 weeks. Results suggested that Reality Therapy seemed to work because it provided strength just where prisoners were weak i.e. if focused on the way life was rather than on a fantasy world, it stressed realistic future goals rather than past failures.

Yarish Paul (1985) in "Reality Therapy and the locus of control of juvenile offenders" studied 45 male juvenile offenders (aged 12-16 years) to determine whether positive perceptual changes could be brought about by the use of Wiiliam Glasser's (1965) therapeutic technique of Reality Therapy. The Nowicki-strickland Locus of Control Scale for children (1973) was administered to students during their 1st and last week in a treatment facility. Evaluation by a matched pairs t-test showed a significant difference between the treatment and control groups. Proponents of locus of control orientation by J.B. Rotter (1966) believed that persons with an internal mechanism of control perceive that events were contingent on their own behaviour, rather than on the powerful control of other students who received Reality Therapy, moved in an internal direction and choose to behave better with control of their fate in their own hands.

Ross (1989) in "Education of the young offenders" - described the program offered by the shaw bridge youth Centre High School for adolescents offenders and focused on the school's life skill and Work Orientation Department, (known by the student as co-op.) overall goals of the educational programs matched to individual needs, and facilitating transaction of students between institutional life and the community. The co-op. was based on the approaches of Reality Therapy. The co-op. program was designed to help students acquire skills to improve their level of autonomy and employability.

Dempster (1990) in "Managing students in Primary schools - A successful Australian Experience" presents a policy of effective student management in Australian schools that was based on the principles of Reality Therapy and control theory.

The author discussed the needed ingredients for program success for the students (aged 5-12 yrs.) the benefits for children of accepting responsibility for one's own behaviour and the benefits for the teachers of the stress reduction that flows from the proper implementation of the program.

Slowick (1991) in "The effects of Reality Therapy Process on locus of Control and self-concepts among Mexican American adolescents" determined the effects of the Reality Therapy process and use of class meeting on Mexican adolescents (7th and 9th graders) perceptions of internal & external locus of control (LOC) and self-concept. 26 students received Reality Therapy (experimental group) 30 students did not (control group) Tools (e.g. the dimensions of self-concept-Forms) were administered 1 week before and 11 weeks after the experiment started. Multivariate Analysis of Variance (MANOVA) indicated that experimental students had significantly higher scores on academic interest, leadership and initiative measures and lower scores on the anxiety measure. However students did not differ significantly on Locus of Control. Students given Reality Therapy were more interested and satisfied with the experiences in school.

Omizo (1992) in "The effects of Reality Therapy classroom meetings on self-concept and locus of control among learning disabled children" presented 60 learning disabled (LD) children aged (12-14 years) from 4 classrooms were randomly assigned to experimental and control conditions. Experimental group teachers were trained by a certified Reality Therapist in the concepts of Reality Therapy and how to conduct the classroom meetings. Students were administered the Dimensions of self-concept (DSC) and Nowicki Strickland Locus of Control

Scale for children. MANCVA yielded no significant differences between the experimental & control groups. The intervention study appeared to be beneficial in improving some aspects of self concept among the learning disabled population.

Fuller (1989) in "Reality Therapy helping Learning Disabled Children to make better Choices" presented 10 step school wide approach based on Reality Therapy and positive teacher student involvement for dealing with learning disabled students. It was concluded that the approach offered everyone involved a chance to work together rather than against one another.

Marandola (1991) in "Glasser's Classroom meeting - a humanistic approach to behaviour change with pre-adolescent learning disabled children" evaluated the effects of Glasser's class-room meeting (William Glasser, 1965, 1969) on the argumentative behaviour of 10-11 years old learning disabled boys. The result of intervention suggested that the method may be effectively used with a learning disabled population.

Knudson (1979) in "Counselling disabled individuals using a Reality Therapy Model" discussed the application of a Reality Therapy paradigm for counseling disabled clients.

John (1986) in "the effects of a program of Behaviour Modification and Reality Therapy on the Behaviour of Emotionally disturbed Institutionalized Adolescents" presented institutionalised staff used behaviour modification and Reality Therapy to bring about positive behaviour changes in 20 severely retarded emotionally disturbed adolescents as measured on two adapative behaviour scales.

Ziegler (1983) discussed the effectiveness of a course in Reality Therapy consisting of six participants. Result indicated that there was increased evidence of mutual trust among members of the group.

Grimesey (1991) described modifications in a middle school's discipline program based on Reality Therapy including ways in which teachers could maintain relationship with students without administrative referrals. Survey data from 37 teachers indicated that most had positive perceptions of the program particularly with their ability to use questions to lead students to identify the problem, judge their own behaviour and develop a plan.

Hart-Hester-Susan (1989) examined the effects of Reality Therapy on the on-task behaviour of participating students across two instructional settings. Four samples aged 9-11 years met with an educational psychologist, formally trained in Reality Therapy for 30-45 minute sessions. Results indicated that Reality Therapy was effective in increasing the on-task behaviour of targeted samples.

Schmidt (1984) discussed the frequent lack of responsibility in students toward learning and toward each other based on three case studies. Conditions in modern society that undermine motivation for responsible behaviour were analyzed. Reality Therapy and the development of positive personality traits were examined. Reality Therapy was very useful to develop a sense of responsibility was emphasized.

Welch (1980) examined the influence of inservice training
in William Glasser's (1965, 1972) Reality Therapy and class
meeting, techniques on teacher affective behaviour, student
on-task behaviour absences. The sample consisted of 8 volun-
tary target teachers. No significant changes in teacher and/or
student behaviour resulted from the in-service training.

Shearn (1978) examined the Reality Therapy method in the
classroom via 94 group experimental design samples were 150,
4th graders in an overseas dependents school system in Japan.

The groups were as follows :-

(a)  Pre-tested Reality Therapy.
(b)  Unpretested Reality Therapy.
(c)  Pretested placebo.
(d)  Unpretested placebo.

The result indicated positive result.

Thompson (1976) described research support for the application of Reality Therapy to the resolution of classroom
discipline problem in the elementary school. Data confirmed
that trained teachers could successfully use Reality Therapy
to reduce the frequency of undesirable pupil behaviour and to
increase the frequency of desirable behaviour.

Dalbech (1981) described the use of Reality Therapy in
groups of 4 students of junior high school. That group
counselling programm had worked well in the school environment.

Meyer (1973) described the development and successful result of an incentive system based on William Glasser's Reality Therapy for use in a residential institution for adolescents adjusted neglected and dependent.

Cobb (1992) described a day long class aimed at helping adolescents in grade 7-12, to increase their self-confidence, acquire self-help tools for coping with everyday challenges and gain more effective control of their lives. The class was based on major components of William Glasser's (1984) Reality Therapy.

Parish (1992) discussed ways to enhance the motivation of students in the context of William Glasser's (1990) control theory and Reality Therapy.

McIntosh (1991) discussed a program called sex and total behaviour that was designed to introduce adolescents to control theory & Reality Therapy.

Acklin (1989) described a special college secretarial curriculum that was supported by Reality Therapy based training to help participants to build their skills in gaining a greater degree of interpersonal understanding & control in their lives.

Banmen (1985) studied William Glasser's concepts of Reality Therapy to explain the dynamics taking place in youth and young adults when they did not accept responsibility and to determine which intervention startegies need to be used to help youth with their career choices and work effectiveness.

81

From all the studies mentioned above one could understand
that the overall goal of Reality Therapy is to find more
effective ways of meeting one's needs for belonging, power
freedom and fun.  The therapeutic process of Reality Therapy
consists of helping students to learn ways to regain control
on their lives and to live more effectively.  These include
confronting students to examine what they are doing, thinking
and feeling to figure out if there is a better way for them
to function, Glasser (1989) emphasized "the only person's
behaviour that we can control is our own, which means that the
best way to control events around us is through what we do.

CHAPTER : III

METHODOLOGY

## 3.1 Introduction :

In this chapter the investigator has detailed out the process and procedures which she has adopted while carrying out study in order to achieve the particular objectives specified below. The methodological procedures adopted are presented in the sections that follow.

## 3.2 Objectives :

a) To prepare a programme of psychological education based on William Glasser's Reality Therapy.

b) To study the effectiveness of Reality Therapy in bringing about changes in students with respect to the following major components of their academic as well as psychological development.

   a)  Assertiveness.
   b)  Sense of Responsibility.
   c)  Attitude toward school.
   d)  Educational Aspiration.
   e)  Academic Achievement.
   f)  Self concept.

## 3.3 Hypotheses of the study:

In the light of the concept of Reality Therapy presented earlier and the objectives stated above, the following Research Hypotheses were generated regarding the effectiveness of the Reality Therapy Intervention programme. When the teacher understands the students, when the students see themselves accepted

83

and valued, they begin to regain their lost powers, and as a
result improve their academic performance, discover their
hidden talents and thus become confident. This also could
bring about better co-operation with their peers and a feeling
of belongingness to the group. They develop positive ways of
looking at things around them and the learning experience thus
turn out to be a satisfying one. The present study attempts
to test some of these hypotheses. The following research
hypotheses have been stated for the present study.

Students' behaviour in respect of -

a) Assertiveness
b) Sense of Responsibility
c) Attitude toward school
d) Educational Aspiration
e) Academic Achievement
f) Self-concept.

before and after the intervention orienting the group along a
Reality Therapy perspective will differ.

3.4 The Design :

The present investigation is an intervention study and
the approach is developmental in nature. The study aims at
evaluating the effects of the intervention of the sample.
Therefore, the investigator thought that the time series design
is most apt for the purpose of the present study.

The Time-series researches are represented as "a set of
observations taken at specified times usually at equal intervals" (Spiegal, 1978) The time series design is of great
significance to the present researcher for the reasons given
below :-

a) It helps in understanding past behaviour- By observing data over a period of time one can easily understand what changes have taken place such analyses will be extremely helpful in predicting the future behavior.

b) It helps in planning future operations - plans for the future cannot be made without forecasting events and relationships they will have statistical techniques have been evolved which enable time series to be analysed in such a way that the influences which have determined the form of that series may be ascertained. If the regularity of occurence of any feature over a sufficient long period could be clearly established, then within its limit prediction of probable future variations would become possible.

c) It helps in evaluating current accomplishment - The actual performance can be compared with the expected performance and the cause of variation analysed. Time series analysis will enable us to apply the scientific procedures of holding other things constant as we examine one variable at a time.

d) It facilitates comparison - Different time series are often compared and important conclusions drawn therefrom.

However, one should not be led to believe that by time series analyses one can fore tell with hundred percent accuracy the course of future events. This could be possible only if the influence of the various forces which affect these series would have been regular in their operation.

The basic outline of the design may be summarised as follows :-

$$O_1 \quad O_2 \quad O_3 \quad \ldots \quad I \quad \ldots \quad O_4 \quad O_5 \quad O_6$$

Base line data                    intervention effects

O = Observation
I = Intervention

Figure : 1 - Basic outline of the design of the study.

The measurement for most of the dependant variables were made thrice before the intervention to see the baseline data  and thrice after the intervention to determine the intervention effect.  The observations were repeated with an interval of four full weeks.

### 3.5  The sample :

For the present study thirty students have been selected from three English medium schools of Baroda city, ten students from each school in the academic year 1993-94.

Vadodara, formerly known as Baroda, used to be one of the more progressive princely states of India.  It had a walled inner city which was the centre of residential and trade activities.  The demographic composition of the city was mainly restricted to Gujarati and Marathi speaking families and it is now a major city of the Gujarat state and a busy metropolis of India.

The three schools from which the samples have been drawn
are :- Rosary School, Fatehgunj, Baroda High School, Alkapuri
and M.G.M. School, New Sama Road respectively.

Rosary school of Baroda is one of the old school of the city.
It is a high school managed by the society of Jesus and recog-
nised and aided by the Department of Education, Gujarat State.
It is co-educational high school. Though a catholic institution
it welcomes pupils of all castes and creeds and prepares them
for the secondary school certificate and the higher secondary
school certificate examination of the two Boards of Education
of the Gujarat State.

Mar Gregorios' Memorial School (M.G.M.) Baroda was established in 1981 and is managed by Mr Gregorios Orthodox Syrian
Church, Baroda. It is a co-educational school and prepares students for the Gujarat State Secondary school Examination. It is
also a co-educational school.

Baroda High School, Alkapuri was founded in 1974. It is a
big co-educational school which has two more branches in other
parts of the Baroda city and prepares students for the secondary school certificate and the higher secondary school certificate examination of the two Boards of Education of the Gujarat
state.

These three schools are situated at different parts of the
Baroda city and the students have come from different socio-
economic backgrounds.

The choice of the particular schools for the study was made
because of the principals' appreciation for the kind of study
proposed and their willingness to provide all the necessary

facilities, especially getting the support of the teachers dealing with the particular class (namely standard IX) was made by
the Principals themselves. The sample of subjects for the study
were selected on the basis of the following criteria.

a)  School performance - The students whose academic
    performance is generally low over the last three to
    four years.

b)  Disciplinary problems - students, who without any
    apparent or sufficient reason create disciplinary
    problems in the school.

c)  Opinions of the concerned teachers - opinions of
    different teachers of class IX of the three schools,
    regarding the students' poor academic performance,
    disciplinary problems have been taken. The past
    records of school performances also have been taken
    into consideration.

d)  Personal and informal interview  of the investigator
    with all students of class IX of the three above-
    mentioned schools. The interviews were mostly related
    with questions regarding the student's  home, school,
    peer groups, aspirations, hobbies, interests etc. to
    draw out more first hand information from the students
    themselves and thus to reach a concrete decision
    regarding the choice of students for the intervention
    programme.

3.6 Instruments for quantitative data :

In the present study the following measurement tools were used for quantitative data collection. The necessary particulars regarding each tool are as under :-

a)  Tasneem Naqvi's Assertiveness Scale (AS).
b)  Responsibility Scale for the high school students (RS) made by the investigator.
c)  Lawrence J. Dolan and Marci Moro Enos School Attitude Measure (SAM)
d)  Nageswara Rao's Educational Aspiration Scale (EAS)
e)  Academic Achievement (AA) (Students' Academic Achievement in the form of percentage of marks obtained in the various tests of class VIII and IX)
f)  Rosenberg's Society and Adolescent Self Image Scale (SAS).

(a)  Tasneem Naquvi's Assertiveness Scale (AS) :

This scale was used to measure the assertiveness of the students. The present Assertiveness Inventory has two parts. The first part measures assertive behaviour and the second part measures blocks to acting assertively. In the first part of the inventory some questions have been given. These questions were helpful in assessing one's assertiveness. All that one has to do is to draw a circle around the number that describes one best.

For some questions the assertive end of the scale is at 0, for others it is at 4.0 means No or never, 1 means somewhat or sometimes, 2 means average, 3 means usually or a good deal, 4 means practically always or entirely. The second part of the inventory is in questionnaire form which covers six areas dealing with own angers, authoritarian behaviour, refusing requests, making requests and initiating communication. Items were collected from different sources of literature, bulletins, reports etc.

The scoring procedure of the scale can be available in the appendix - where on the basis of a table the scores can be interpreted.

| Scores | Interpretation |
|---|---|
| 110 - 135 | Practically assertive |
| 91 - 109 | Usually assertive |
| 60 - 90 | Average Assertive |
| 34 - 59 | Non assertive |
| 7 - 33 | Entirely Non-assertive. |

(For the interpretation of the part - 1)

The part 2 is the questionnaire by which one can know blocks to acting assertively.

(b) Responsibility Scale (RS): for the High school students - The Responsibility Scale (RS) was prepared and standardized by the investigator herself. The Scale is comprised of fifteen statements. This scale has been made for class IX students in the age group of 12-15. The objective of this scale is to see whether the student has some sense of responsibility or he/she lacks it. Here the term responsibility has been used in some specific sense. According to the investigator a responsible person is one who thinks about present and future in a consistent way and takes charge of it and also takes charge of his own action and speech. A responsible person can meet his own needs and

also looks after others' needs. He feels that he has some
duty toward his family, school and society and never tries
to deny it. A responsible person has a positive attitude
about himself and his dealings with other is generally
consistent, direct and honest.

The fifteen items of this scale is marked on a four
point scale from strongly agree, Agree, Disagree, Strongly
disagree but they are scored only as agreement or disagreement. This test reports a test-retest reliability
and validity. Items of this scale were collected from
different sources and a group of experts from different
disciplines were consulted regarding weightage for each
category. The maximum score for the scale is ten,
representing high responsibility and the lowest score is
zero, representing no sense of responsibility. The scale
is simple and also easy for administering and scoring.
The maximum time limit taken by the students were ten
minutes.

(c)    Lawrence J. Dolan and Marci Moro Enos School Attitude
       Measure (SAM) :
       The following objectives such as Motivation for schooling,
       Academic Self concept both performance based and reference
       based sense of control over performance and instructional
       mastery were measured by the sub-scales of School Attitude
       Measure. It is a Self-report Survey for school success as
       cognitive ability. The school Attitude Measure comprises
       five sub scales. They are :-

       Sub-scale: A
       Motivation for schooling - It consists of seventeen (17)
       items and is concerned with the effect of students'
       reactions to past school experience upon their motivation

in school. The way students have come to feel about their total school experience can influence how hard they want work in school, how highly they value school, and how much they want to pursue further schooling.

## Sub-scale : B

Academic Self-concept performance based - The Scale items are concerned with the student's confidence in their academic instrument, to provide evaluation of student's affective responses to their school experience. To understand better the performance of students in school, it is useful to examine their perceptions of themselves as competent learners. The affective domain is related to students' attitudes, interests and emotional responses. Based on their experiences in school, students develop both negative and positive affective responses toward many dimensions of school life. These affective responses lead to the crucial perceptions that students form of themselves as learners. These affective responses can be as important abilities, their feelings about their school performance. Students' feelings about their academic abilities can contribute to their success or lack of success in school. This subscale also consists of seventeen (17) items.

## Sub-scale : C

Academic Self-concept - Reference based - The Seventeen (17) statements which comprises this sub-scale are concerned with how students think other people (teacher, family, friends) feel about students' school performance and their ability to succeed academically.

## Sub-scale : D

Students' sense of control over performance - The Statements comprising this sub-scale are concerned with students' feelings about being able to exercise control over situations that affect them at school, like grades and promotions and to take responsibility for them.

## Sub-scale : E

Student's Instructional Mastery - Unlike the first four sub-scales which dealt with student's feeling the items of this sub-scale ask students to report the state of their actual school skills, like their ability to use school time effectively, persistence in instructional tasks, ability to seek and use feedback from others and ability to evaluate their own work.

The SAM is available in three levels, for use with students ranging from grades four through twelve. In the present study level II survey was used. It has a total of Eighty-three (83) items. Each item is marked on a four point scale from never agree to always agree. It reports a test-retest reliability of 0.94 with four weeks apart. SAM is appended under Appendix.

(d) Nageswara Rao's Educational Aspiration Scale (EAS) -

Nageswara Rao's Educational Aspiration Scale was used to measure educational aspiration of the students. This scale was originally constructed and standardized by Dr.R.B. Mathur of RCE, Ajmer (1969). The reported validity of the scale against the opinion of the teachers was 70 and test-retest reliability of .59 (after 26 days) Nageswara Rao (1982) modified this scale. Thus the educational aspiration scale used in this scale was an

adapted version of the original scale. In this scale a
list of seventeen educational plans are listed and students
were asked to select one of them. If their plan does
not fall in any of the category they are asked to specify
it in the eighteenth category. A group of experts from
different states in the society were consulted for their
opinions regarding weightage for each category. The
maximum score for the scale is 9 while minimum is 1. The
scale is simple and also easy for administering and
scoring. The maximum time limit taken by the students
were 10 minutes. The full scale can be found in the
appendix.

(e)  Academic Achievement (AA) -

For measuring Academic Achievement a deliberate decision
was made not to go for standardised achievement tests.
Instead teacher made tests were made use of students'
academic achievement in the form of percentages of marks
obtained in the various tests of standard VIII and IX were
taken as criteria for academic achievement in the present
investigation.

(f)  Rosenberg's Society and Adolescent Self-Image Scale (SAS)-
Students' self-esteem was measured by this scale. The
scale measures the self-acceptance aspect of self-esteem.
It was developed by Rosenberg (1965) for use with high
school students. It is a short scale of ten statements,
compressed into six scales. It is easy to administer.
The items are answered on a four point scale from strongly
agree to strongly disagree but they are scored only as
agreement or disagreement following Guttman Scaling. It
has a test-retest correlation coefficient of 0.85 over

two weeks and Guttman Scale reproducibility co-efficient
of 0.92. The maximum score on the scale is 6, representing high self-esteem and the lowest score is zero,
representing low self-esteem. The scale is appended
under Appendix.

## 3.7 Instruments used for collecting qualitative and descriptive information :

Qualitative data were exploratory in nature, probing into
the "what" and "how" aspects of the various home and social
environmental elements, processes and interactions during the
intervention programme; influencing an urban adolescent students
response to the demands made on him by the formal schooling to
perform and the change that occurs during the intervention
programme and after. These questions could not be answered
conclusively by compartmentalising the phenomenon in terms of
variables expressed in quantitative measures and analysing
their relationships through statistical techniques. What was
called for on the other hand was a more comprehensive and
descriptive information which were qualitative in nature. The
approach here had to be idiographic as opposed to the nomoth-
etic approach selected for establishing causal relationships
among variables. For establishing causal relationships the
approach was to observe the group during intervention elicited
information regarding the distribution of the group on
selected variables and analysing the relationships among them
on the other hand for seeking answers to the other questions
the investigator had gone for a case study approach for a
limited number of students and attempted descriptive surveys
covering their school and home observations and lengthy
interviews involving the student; his parents and significant
others were the main inputs for building each case study.

The following measurement tools were used for qualitative
data collection :-

a)  Interview schedule for students.
b)  Interview schedule for parents.
c)  Case studies.
d)  Anecdotal Records.
e)  Educational Environment at home scale.
f)  Home Interaction pattern scale.
g)  Social competence scale
h)  Behavioural adjustment to the intervention programme.

(a)  Interview schedule :  In order to get more first-hand
information about the learners, the student and their
parents were interviewed.  For this purpose the investigator prepared an interview schedule  for both of the
groups which are appended in the Appendix.

(b)  Case studies :  In order to discover in depth how  the
Reality Therapy Intervention programme in the group has
been operating for individual students, six case studies,
three representing students who showed much gain and
three who had no such gain on some variables studied, and
in the opinion of the investigator based on her classroom observations and personal interviews were conducted.
In order to do the case studies the selected six students
were interviewed for several times.  The investigator also
interviewed their parents.  The items of the student's
interview schedule and parent's interview schedule were
used as lead questions which have been presented in the
Appendix.

(c) <u>Aneedotal Records</u> : Observation as a technique becomes
necessary in recording the classroom procedures during
intervéntion program. This information was not to be
put through the rigours of quantification but was
essential in building the backdrop and identifying the
processes during the intervention programme that was
responsible for their behaviours.

It was thought that a qualitative accounting of the
going on of the class-room would be recorded. Therefore
a day to day observation record of the students during
the intervention program was kept by the investigator.

(d) <u>Educational Environment at home scale</u> : The educational
environment essentially is the support and guidance the
family provides for the education of the child. For the
present study Dave's ( 1963) concept of educational
environment has been taken as a guiding principle to
define the variable "educational environment at home." ₹
The tool has four press variables as the core of the
educational environment at home. They are :-

1. Working habits of the family.
2. Academic guidance and support.
3. Stimulation to explore and discuss.
4. Academic aspirations and expectations.

The full scale is included in the appendix.

(e) <u>Home Interaction Pattern Scale</u> : The home is the Social
arena where on the one hand there is the adolescent boy/
girl with his/her individual capacities, interests and
pre-occupations and on the other hand are the parents or
the adult family members who too have their own individual
capacities, interests, temperaments, frustrations etc.
These two are in a constant interaction with each other.
The parents often attempt to alter the child's behavior
to suit their notion of a good child. These interactions
differ in homes in tune with the parental personalities
and other varying factors like the number of family
members the type of family, the economic level of the
family etc. They also acquire a certain amount of
stability over a given period time fluctuating within a
given range only. There are a number of issues or area
as in which these parent child interaction occur. For
the present study however four crucial aspects of the
interactions were identified. The four aspects were:-

1.   The autonomy given to the child.
2.   The type of disciplining used.
3.   The reinforcement given to the child.
4.   The sibling interaction.

However the full scale is appended in the Appendix.

(f) <u>Social Competence Scale</u> : Social competence refers to the
degree of competence the adolescent exhibits in dealing
with the situations of everyday life in his/her content
of the social environmental milieu.

These situations could be wide ranging. Tackling
personal tasks, social transactions with peers and
adults or even undertaking a task or an activity.   The
social competence here was generally here to be taken as
the initiative the student takes in different spheres of
personal tasks, social interaction with peers and adults
and in play and work.  Also it is the interest and
perseverance with which the adolescent follows age suitable
tasks of work and play.  It was used both as an observation
tool and an interview schedule.  The scale was circulated
to a panel of experts consisting of educationist,
psychologists school teachers and parents.  This was done
to ensure the content validity of the  scale suggested
changes were duly incorporated.  The schedule was
prepared by the investigator.  The full scale is available
in the Appendix.

(g)  <u>Behavioural adjustment to the intervention programme</u> :

This scale is the behavioral adaptation the student made
to the different components of the intervention programme.
.This self-reporting inventory was developed by Youngman
(1969)  Youngman's inventory was essentially used to
describe the typical school behavior and the second
criterion followed by Youngman while framing the items
was that they be as objective as possible.  Youngman's
inventory presently under discussion was arrived at after
administering and factor analysing a 40 items inventory
with 274, 12 years old and 288, nine years olds
secondary school students as the sample.  The Youngman's
inventory was designed to measure the behavioral adjustment to school.  It measured  three specific dimensions.
One the studieusness, two the compliance and three the

teacher contact. All the three sub-scales as well as the total score showed acceptable reliability and well defined construct validity within normal lower secondary population. Youngman further suggested the idea of a teacher form for the scale so that the teacher can assess the children's adjustment rather than rely on self-report-9 more appropriate procedure with students or poor readers. However, the items of the present scale has been taken from Youngman's inventory discussed above. The inventory was in a form of a teacher rating inventory. The full scale has been added in the Appendix.

## 3.8  Intervention :

An intervention programme was prepared by the investigator following the guidelines of Reality Therapy as given by Dr. William Glasser. However the intervention programme has three separate phases.

1st phase :  Involvement with the students by creating a warm and supportive climate in the group.

2nd phase :  knowledge about one's own unrealistic behavior and gradual avoidance of it.

3rd phase :  Learning of Responsible ways to fulfill one's needs within the confines of reality.

## 3.9  Procedural details :

The study was conducted in three phases. Pre-intervention phase, Intervention phase and the Post-Intervention phase. During the pre-intervention phase the investigator ascertained the status of the variables by collecting data three times with a time period of four weeks apart. The procedures in the three school were more or less the same.

On the first day the principal took the investigator to the particular class and introduced her to the students saying that she was a researcher in the "Centre of Advanced Study in Education" and that she wanted to conduct an educational programme in the class. The investigator then added that this educational programme was introduced by Dr.William Glasser a famous educationist in the United States of America. It is a very effective programme for the school students to bring out their hidden qualities and to make them a successful person in every sense. She also told that she is the first person to introduce this programme in India and for this purpose she has selected three schools in Baroda to conduct the programme. She told the students that she wanted to make learning an enjoyable experience for students. Afterwards she added that for the time being she would select 10 students from the class.

After the selection of students the investigator expressed her intention to get to know each one of them, their interests and the kind of difficulties they face in the class. During the pre intervention period the investigator familiarized herself with the students informally during recess time.

After having enough involvement with the students for a month or so, the investigator administered the different data gathering instruments on the students and repeated them two times more with a time gap of four weeks apart. However the Responsibility Scale was administered on the students two times before the intervention and the instruments for qualitative data were administered once during the intervention period.

The procedural details of different scales administration for quantitative data in the pre-intervention phase are as follows:-

(a) Assertiveness Scale :

The investigator read aloud and explained the meaning of all items of the Assertiveness Inventory. She then told the students to go through all the items first to get a clear perception of the scale, and then to mark the items according to the instruction as was given in the front page of the scale.

(b) Responsibility Scale :

Cyclostyled copies of the scale were distributed to the students. The investigator explained the meaning of all the items of the scale to the students and instructed them to mark the items according to the instruction given to them.

(c) School Attitude Measure :

Copies of the test were distributed to the student and they were explained the marking procedure. The investigator read the 83 statements of the inventory and cleared the meaning where the students were facing problems.

(d) Educationa Aspiration Scale :

The students were given a copy of the Educational Aspiration Scale. They were asked to write their name age, class and the name of the school in the respective space provided for them. After allowing the students sufficient time to go through the items of the scale, the investigator told the students to mark any one item of the scale. She also told the students that if he/she didn't find any

of the item suiting his/her choice, he/she can write his/
her specific choice at the empty space provided at the
end of the scale.

(e) Academic Achievement :

Percentage of marks obtained by the sample of students
in the various tests of standard VIII and IX were taken
as criteria for determining academic achievement in the
pre and post-intervention phase.

(f) Rosenberg's Self-esteem scale :

Cyclostyled copies of the Scale were distributed to the
students and they were asked to fill in their names and
other details as required. The investigator read aloud
the instruction and illustrated the procedure for marking
before they were asked to mark the scale. The items
were read to the student to check if they clearly understood them before they were asked to mark the scale.

Regarding the instruments which were used for gathering
qualitative data were used during the Intervention
period. The procedures of administration for all those
scales were as follows.

Cyclostyled copies of the scale were distributed to the
students. The investigator explained the meaning of all
the items of the scale to the students and instructed
them to mark the items according to the instruction given
to them.

However the Intervention programme went for one full
academic year that is 1993 to 1994. After the Intervention
programme the scales used for quantitative data were used
three times with a gap of one full month between each administration.

Interview schedule -

Once during the pre-intervention phase and once during
the post intervention phase each student was interviewed
individually. The interviews were held during the school hours.
The interview schedule for the parents were sent to them
through their wards.

Case Studies :

Six students were chosen to study indepth. Their choice
was done applying the following criteria: one student from each
group who gained a great deal in all criterion measures like
assertiveness, sense of responsibility, positive attitude
toward school, educational aspiration, academic achievement and
self-esteem and in the overall judgement at the investigator
which she arried at as a result of her months of observations
and interaction during the experimentation period and during
the interviews. Similarly one student from each group was
identified from among those who did not do well in the above
criteria.

3.10 Data Analysis :

The data thus collected being both quantitative and qualitative were subjected to both quantitative and qualitative
analyses.

However, for quantitative data, the Means, standard Deviations and Frequency Distributions of each variables of all the

six observations were computed. Again the t-tests were conducted to determine the levels of difference among successive data points, separated by different time intervals in the series. The data were then transformed into line graphs using means of observation and were plotted over different intervention phase.

For qualitative data the group processes during the intervention programme were recorded in detail without using any structured observation schedule. Class-room incidents as they occurred were faithfully recorded using aneedotal recording technique. The six children were selected on the basis of their achievement on the selected variable. Three of them were high achivers and three low achievers in all the variables. Unstructured interviews were conducted with those students and through a series of scales and inventory administration case study reports were prepared for each of these six children.

A detailed analyses of data and the results are presented in chapter - V.

3.11  The chapters to follow :

The design of the present study discussed in this chapter clearly indicates that the methodology of collecting empirical evidences to answer the hypotheses are both quantitative and qualitative. The subsequent chapters therefore are organised according to this scheme. In the fourth chapter various materials are developed by the Investigator or drew up by her from various sources for intervention for the students to orient them on the Reality Therapy perspective. This chapter however has been titled as "Materials developed and used for intervention". The processing of quantitative data, the analytical procedures adopted and an interpretative discussion are presented in the chapter five entitled "Data Analyses". Chapter Six (6) ties up the loose ends of both the quantitative and $\wedge$ *qualitative data* and discusses the emerging composite reality. This chapter is called summary and conclusion.

CHAPTER : IV

MATERIALS DEVELOPED AND USED FOR INTERVENTION

4.1  Introduction :

Presented in this chapter are the various materials, developed by the Investigator or drew up by her from various sources
for intervention for the students, to orient them on the Reality
Therapy perspective.

Ist Phase

4.2  Involvement with the students : by creating a warm and
supportive climate in the group

From the first day of the intervention programme, the
investigator tried to creat a warm and supportive environment
in the group.

However, involvement with the students was not a goal in
itself, but a means to an end action and as the investigator
used high levels of attending, accurate empathy, genuineness,
respect and concreteness, the students cooperated by exploring
their feelings, experiences and behaviors related to the
problematic areas of their life. The investigator used a variety
of skills to help the students understand themselves more fully
in order to see the need to act more effectively. She not only
helped the students to join together the data produced through
self-exploration process, so that they could see a bigger
picture, a theme or a pattern in their life, but also helped
them probe wider and look deeper in order to find the missing

pieces they need, to understand themselves better. Once the students began to see themselves both as they were and as they wanted to be, they saw the necessity for action. The goal of this stage was dynamic, that is self-understanding, as genuinely and concretely as possible.

In stage II the investigator tried to see the world from the students' frame of reference. In this stage, she helped the students to see the world from a more objective point of view.

The III stage was a bridge between the stage I and stage II. From the point of view of self-understanding, in this final stage, the investigator lead the students to a pathway of constructive behavioural change.

In the first phase the investigator took time to get involved with the students, only as much as she was comfortable with them. The reason was that if she tried too hard and went too fast, the students might interpret that what she was doing as over-selling and might doubt her sincerity and as the students were not accustomed to this type of approach they might interpret too much effort on the part of the investigator as coercive and the whole programme might be ineffective.

When the investigator was sure that the time was ready, she explained clearly and specifically her programme. She convinced the students by saying that there would be no threats, punishments or busy works in that special group and that she would not ask the students to learn or do anything that were not useful to them. She emphasized that the students should feel at ease and could discuss about their problems in the group, no matter how small it was.

The investigator also added that she would meet the students twice a week, one hour for each day and the sessions would continue till the end of their academic year.

The investigator then looked for natural occassions to tell the students about herself. The investigator made an effort as much as possible to help her students to know her and to trust her. The investigator's main aim was that the students would know her well enough and would like what they know about her, so that they would see her as the best person they had ever met beside their families, and as the students got to know the investigator, they would gain much of the closeness and they in turn revealed more and more about themselves that was needed. The investigator tried to convince her students that something new and better for them was happening and the students were encouraged to talk honestly and easily to the investigator and she to them.

The following were the things which the investigator discussed with the students.

a) <u>Who she is</u>

Her name, her family, the members of her family, her native state, special characteristics of the city where she was dwelling, her house, her neighbourhood, her friend circle, her education, school, college, university, her teachers, her food habit, her favourite food, her favourite T.V. programme, her special interest, her hobby etc.

b) <u>What she stands for</u>

Her values, did she read books - what were they - Did she has a stand on what was going on in India - for example about the riots in the cities, and what would she

do about them if she had a chance to do something. Did
she disagree with her parents - her friends - and what
did she do when she disagree. Did she vote and what did
she do to find out who to vote for. Did she think grades
are important and if not what were more important in
school etc.

c)  What she will ask the students to do

The investigator then told the students that she was
going to ask them to work with her to solve any problem
that arose in their group and outside the group. But
the investigator also made it clear that she was much
more interested in them solving their own problems than
doing it for them. She also told the students that the
purpose of that group was to teach them, how to use what
they had learnt and that she would expect them to be
able to show her that they were able to do that.

d)  What she will do for them

As long as the students come to that group, the
investigator helped them in anyway she could. The
investigator gave the impression that she was their
friend and that she was always on their side, it would
never be she against them. For example when the students
needed more time to figure something out or to do a
better job, she gave that to them or advised them to do
it at home or in the library. When they had questions,
the investigator either answered them or found someone
who could. When they had any problem in their lives the
investigator tried to help but most of what she helped
them with, was limited to school. The investigator

conducted group meetings, whenever the students thought
there was anything that need discussions and encouraged
the students to speak out. The investigator never threa-
tened, punished or put down anyone at any time. At the
same time the investigator told them that she was not
perfect and if they found that she was not doing as she
said, the students should not be afraid to tell her and
the investigator would either explain or change.

e)  What she will not do for them

The investigator did not do their work or figure out
any problem for the students. The investigator did not
tell them what to do if she could understand that the
students could figure out the problems for themselves.
The investigator spent a lot of time teaching them how
to evaluate their own work. Once they would know how to
do that, the investigator expected them to do those by
themselves and would learn to defend the evaluation of
their work by others. The investigator explained to the
students that to be successful in life we must evaluate
ourselves and would work to improve. We could not and
should not depend on others to do that for us.

Next the investigator led the group through the
following group exercises.

Through all those exercises in all the three phases
of the intervention programme the investigator wanted to
make the students aware that quality work was what she
wanted from them and that in her group they could achieve
that.

## 4.3  Session - I : Ice-breaking

### Objective :

Mutual introduction, get to know one another well, learn to talk about one-self.

### Procedure :

The purpose of this ice-breaking session was that each and every members of the group had enough idea about other group members and so that there would be proper involvement among them.

The investigator asked each individual student to intro-duce himself/herself in the group. The investigator told the students that they could tell about their parents and family. They might also tell about their personal progress, their future plans and life goals.

The investigator invited someone to begin. After the first speaker, the order of the speaker was random. The investigator encouraged the students by saying

    Think who are you ?
    What are your real self ?
    What are you going to be ?
    Why do you want to become that ?

### Debriefing :

The session was followed by students sharing their own experiences.

## 4.4 Session - 2 : Sharing experiences :

Objective :

    To share one's experience with others, and thus getting closer to each other.

Procedure :

    The investigator then asked the group members to select a partner with whom they would like to discuss on given topics. Once the pairs were formed the following instructions were given to the students.

    The investigator told that only one member of the pair will be allowed to speak for 2 minutes while other partner had to listen attentively without interrupting.

    After two minutes the other partner would talk on the selected topic.

    After five minutes the students were called back and to take their respective seats. Then each member of the group was asked to narrate what his partner had talked about. The topics suggested by the investigator to hold conversation, were as follows.

    a)    Share one of the most significant experience that you could recollect from your childhood.

    b)    What memories would bring you the most pleasure/ most pain.

    c)    Describe one thing that you did on your own initiative, but the result was depressing and your're really ashamed of it.

d) Describe one event when someone seriously misunder-
stood you.

e) What did you usually day dream
Why did you do it ?

f) What was your favourite game ?
What did you like in that game ?

g) Tell your partner about your favourite film/T.V.
serial and what did you like about it

h) Find out the common interests between yourselves.
Ask your partner what he thought were your two
strengths and two weakness.

i) Tell your partner two things - you liked in him and
two things you did not appreciate in him.

Debriefing :

The session was followed by students sharing their
experiences.

4.5 Session No.3 - Make telephone calls :

Objective :

To make group members more involved with each other.

Procedure :

The group members formed pairs and pretend that both of
the members of a pair were on the opposite ends of a telephone
line. The pair were given one problem and they both solved

one problem another pair was given the next chance. All the
procedures were taken place in front of the group. The
following problems were given to solve.

    a)    Your house was on fire.
    b)    Your cat got stuck on a tree.
    c)    A friend fall and broke his hand.
    d)    You wanted to know what time a Movie starts.
    e)    You had left your homework at your friend's place.
    f)    There was a lion in your backyard which had been
        escaped from the zoo.

## Debriefing :

The session was followed by students sharing their own
experiences.

## 4.6 Session - 4 : All about me and my feelings :

## Objective :

To help the students to know more about themselves and
their feelings and to get more involved with the group.

## Procedure :

The group members were asked to write a few lines on each
topic as mentioned under. The students wrote atleast one
paragraph on each topic and after writing all the topics, they
shared those topics in the group.

The topics were as follow :-

   a)   I like having you (the investigator) in my group because _____

   b)   In my school I like to _____

   c)   When I would grow up I would _____

   d)   I got mad when _____

   e)   I'm happy when _____

## Debriefing :

The session was followed by students sharing their own experiences.

## 4.7 Session - 5 : Describe a friend

## Objective :

To help the student to involve him/her in the small group to have experience in talking infront of a group beginning with one to one peer conversation and thus gradually increase his/her self-confidence.

## Procedure :

One individual student chose another student from the group as a partner and looked carefully at the partner, thought of ways to describe him/her and wrote as many things as he/she could about the partner. The procedure was repeated

by the partner. Each individual student described two other
classmates and the procedure was same as before. All members
of the group ended the session by telling to the group
I'm glad to be me because _____
and described one partner by saying

You are glad to be you because _____

## Debriefing :

The session was followed by students sharing their own
experiences.

## 4.8  Session - 6 : Role Play

## Objective:

To enable the students to realize that a role-free expre-
ssion of self is satisfying to self and others.

## Procedure:

The investigator asked the group to form into pairs. She
told them that they were going to do some role plays. One of
the pairs would be A and the other B.

After playing the particular role the player switched the
role and continued playing.  The situations were -

    a)    Somebody called you a bad name.
    b)    Nobody would play with you at recess.
    c)    You had a nightmare last night.

d)    Your friend received a new game and you did not.
e)    Your pet died.
f)    Your teacher didn't choose you for the game.

Debriefing :

The session was followed by students sharing their own experiences.

4.9  Session - 7 : Friendship circle

Objective :

To develop the sense of self-worth and positive self concept and to be more open infront of the group.

Procedure :

The investigator discussed with the students what the word friendly means. She then placed some cards in the middle of the circle of the students with the following writings :

a)    Your friend pushed you down at recess.
b)    A classmate helped you with your work.
c)    Someone took the ball away from you.
d)    A person smiled at you.
e)    A classmate told you that he doesn't like you.
f)    A friend invited you over to her house to play.
g)    You were sick, and someone made you a get well card.
h)    A close friend forgot your birthday.

i)   Someone shared his snack with you.

j)   A friend told you that she liked your work.

The investigator then divided the group into two teams.  Each
team then picked a card read that aloud and decided if the
statement described a way to be friendly.  The team then
decided whether the statement depicted an unfriendly action -
the investigator then asked the group why they thought the
action was unfriendly and sought the group's help to correct
the sentence, so  that described a friendly action.

### Debriefing :

The session was followed by students sharing their own
experiences.

### 4.10 Session - 8 :  A why to live for

### Objective:

To get more knowledge about one's own life.

### Procedure:

The investigator asked the students to write in their
notebook what she  dictates and then write the answer for it.
When everybody's writing was complete then everybody shared
his/her experience in the group.  The following questions were
given to the students :-

a)   Do you believe that a person needs something or
     someone to live for _____?

b)   Why do you think that _____

c)   List some tasks you have done or observed other
     people do that donot seem to make sense because
     they lack meaning

     a)   Tasks with little or no meaning _____
     b)   No meaning because _____
     c)   Tasks with much meaning _____
     d)   Have meaning because _____

## Debriefing :

The session was followed by students sharing their own
experiences.

## IInd Phase

4.11 Knowledge about one's own unrealistic behavior and
gradual avoidance of it :

After having enough involvement and emotional rapport with
the students, the investigator started the second phase of the
intervention programme.

Now the investigator asked to herself :-

1.   What are the problemetic behavior that each of these
     students exhibited ?

2.   What need or needs are they trying to satisfy with
     those behaviors ?

3.   What suggestions will make sense to the students ?

4.   Will they try out the suggestions ?

Keeping in mind all the above mentioned questions the
investigator gave some  selected exercises to the students,
so that step by step they would come to know about the defects
in their own behavior and through the constant feedback which
investigator gave them throughout the course, the students
learn ways to get rid of all these defects.

4.12 Session No.1 - Trait Checklist :

Objective :

To become aware of one's own characteristics and to get
rid of unwanted behaviours.

Procedure :

The investigator provided each student with a questionnaire and asked them to use a check mark ( _/ ) beside those statements that fit his/her self-image. She also told them to use a cross ( X ) to mark those statements that didnot fit his/her self-image and to use a question mark ( ? ) to indicate the one  that they are unsure about -

The questionnaire follows :-

a) _____ Like Myself.
b) _____ Afraid of or hurt by others.
c) _____ People can trust me.
d) _____ Put up a good front.
e) _____ Usually say the right thing.
f) _____ Feel bad about myself.
g) _____ Fearful of the future.
h) _____ Dependent on others for ideas.
i) _____ Waste time.
j) _____ Use my talents.
k) _____ Think for myself.
l) _____ Know my feelings.
m) _____ Don't understand myself.
n) _____ Feel hemmed in.
o) _____ Use time well.
p) _____ Can't hold a job.
q) _____ Trust myself.
r) _____ Usually say the wrong thing.
s) _____ Enjoy people .
t) _____ Don't enjoy being the sex I am.
u) _____ Discouraged about life.
v) _____ Don't like to be around people.

122

w) _____ Havenot develop my talents.
x) _____ Competent in my work.
y) _____ People avoid me.
z) _____ Can't control my emotion.

After the marking was over the investigator told the students
to look at those traits that they had marked in order to
discover a pattern. After the students' observation the
investigator gave some more questionnaire to the students to
help them to change the ineffective pattern of their life.

a) How do you feel about yourself.       Loser/Winner

b) How do you feel about what you
   accomplished in your life            Loser/Winner

c) Are you satisfied with where
   you placed yourself _____

d) If not what would you like to
   change _____

Defriefing:

   After the exercise was over, each student reported what
he or she felt while giving answers to all of those questions
and what was satisfying or not satisfying about them.

4.13 Session No.2 - Learning from your projection :

Objective ;

   To have better self-knowledge.

## Procedure :

The investigator told the students visualize someone whom you particularly dislike and write the answers of the following questions.

a)   What are the things I do not like about that person ?

b)   Do I know others who possesses similar traits ? Do I also dislike them ?

Now raise the question could it possible be true that I do the same thing.

Again the investigator told the students :-

Visualize someone whom you particularly admire and write the answers of the following questions.

a)   What are the things I like about that person.

b)   Do I know others who possesses similar traits.

c)   Do I also admire those people.

The investigator then told the students, now raise the question could it possibly be true that I had the potentiality to actually do and be those things myself.

The investigator again added for one week keep two separate lists. On one list write down all the things you accused others of, on the other list keep track of all the statements of admiration you made of the person, whom you respect.

Do you see any pattern ? Now raise the question - could it possibly be true that I.........................

Debriefing :

The session was followed by students sharing their own experiences.

4.14  Session No.3  - What to let go :

Objective :

To get rid of one's unwanted behavior.

Procedure :

The investigator told the students to list those things about you, that you would like to get rid of or would like to have changed in some way.  Then write the answers of the following questions.

a)     Things I want to let go of.
b)     How to start letting go.
c)     Write about some situations in your life when faced a challenge to change yourself.  When you needed courage and may have felt inadequate to that challenge.  How did it work out ?
d)     As a planner I see myself adequate/inadequate.
e)     The kind of plans I make are often_____
f)     I think this is because I _____
g)     Generally speaking I am/am not satisfied with my planning abilities.  What I want to improve about my planning is _____

Debriefing:

The session was followed by, students sharing their own experiences.

4.15      Session No.4 - Breaking out of bash trap :

Objective :

    To help the students to come out of the trapped situation
of their life.

Procedure :

    The investigator told the students if they feel trapped
in any area of their lives, they could try the following
fantasy exercise.

    Close your eyes and fantasize you're bashing your head
against a high brick wall, trying to get something on the
other side.

    Try to find some way to get over, under or around the
wall without bashing

    a)    If you need something for help, you invent it.
    b)    Imagine several ways of getting out of the trap.
    c)    Write down different possible ways of getting
           out of it.

Debriefing :

    The session was followed by students sharing their own
experiences.

4.16    Session No.5 - Adult ethics :

Objective :

    To help the students become aware of moral/social values.

Procedure :

    The investigator told the students to write down the answers of the following questions and share it in the graoup.

a)   Who and what do I value ?
b)   Who and what do I live for ?
c)   What is really important to me ?
d)   What do I want to be today ? _____

    i)  In 5 years ? _____
    ii) In 10 years ? _____

e)   What potentials do I have for becoming that person ?
f)   What are the barriers ?
g)   What are the alternatives ?

Debriefing :

    The session was followed by students sharing their own experiences.

4.17    Session No.6 - Self Revealation :

Objective :

    To help the students to become aware of themselves (their good points as well as bad points in their nature) through the answering of the following questions.

Procedure :

The investigator told the students ask yourselves the following questions. Took time to reflect and note down your answers and share it in the group.

- a) What is there about me that I like myself ?
- b) What is there about me that I don't like ?
- c) What is there about me that could make other persons to like me ?
- d) What is there about me that would make other persons to dislike me ?
- e) What is there in me that my parents like to see ?
- f) What is there in me that my parents don't like from me ?

Debriefing :

The session was followed by students, sharing their own experiences.

4.18      Session No.7 - Group meetings :

Objective :

To solve behavioral educational problems.

Procedure :

The students sat in a semi-circle facing the investigator and each aww had hisn turn to speak. If the student had nothing he wanted to say he had the right to pass. There were three types of meetings all of which were designed to provide the student with a feeling of involvement and success.

In the open-ended meetings the students discussed questions related to their lives or the curriculum. These meetings were designed to promote educational relevance by dealing with intellectually important topics. Factual answers were not
sought instead theinvestigator attempted to stimulate the students to think.

The second type of meeting was the social problem solving meeting which attempted to solve social problems of the school itself. While school often encourages students to apply their intelligence to the solution of academic problems, it rarely provides students with opportunities to apply their intelligence to the solution of personal and social problems confronting them. But the social problem solving meeting helped children to learn more effective ways of coping with dilemmas.

Either students or the investigator brought up problems for discussion. The discussion was always directed toward solving the problem. The solution did not include punishment or assessment or blame. The purpose was always positive, to find better ways to behave.

These meetings were not held nearly as often as open-ended meetings and they lasted from 30 to 45 minutes. Sample topics included truancy loneliness, class bullies and respect for others.

The purpose of the meeting was to find solutions and not who was at fault.

The third type of meeting, the educational diagnostic meetings were closely related to topics that the group was currently studying.

All these three types of meetings helped to bridge the gap between the group procedures and everyday life. Moreover, students gained the important belief that they could shape their own destinies and they were a vital part of their world. Also the students developed confidence as a result of stating their opinion before a group.

Debriefing :

The session was followed by students sharing their own experiences.

Basing on the information acquired during the first two phases of involvement, the investigator made a list of major area of difficulty of 30 individual students. The diagnostic table of problems gave her a clear insight about the students' problems and helped her a lot in arranging the exercises of IIIrd and the final stage of the program "The Relearning" However the investigator tried her best to pinpoint the main problem of an individual student. It is needless to say that in many cases one student suffered from more than one problems.

4.19  —  Diagnostic Table of Problems

School - I

| Students | Problems |
| --- | --- |
| No.1 | Anxious about school performance. |
| No.2 | Lonely and depressed. |
| No.3 | Emotionally disturbed. |
| No.4 | Learning problem. |
| No.5 | Silent and withdrawn. |
| No.6 | Noisy. |
| No.7 | Irresponsible. |
| No.8 | Short attention span. |
| No.9 | Inefficient in decision making |
| No.10 | Low work out-put/s slowness. |

130

## School - II

| Students | Problems |
|---|---|
| No.1 | Lazy |
| No.2 | Lacks self-respect |
| No.3 | Test Phobia |
| No.4 | Wants attention |
| No.5 | Has problem in aprticipating in class-room discussions. |
| No.6 | Has no idea about constructive use of time. |
| No.7 | Underachiever |
| No.8 | Lacks self-control |
| No.9 | Inefficient in decision making |
| No.10 | Afraid of speaking in a group. |

## School - III

| Students | Problems |
|---|---|
| No.1 | Inappropriate study Habit |
| No.2 | Non-assertive |
| No.3 | Lacks educational aspiration |
| No.4 | Negative attitude toward school |
| No.5 | Dependent on others for decision making & problem solving. |
| No.6 | Lacking in self-esteem. |
| No.7 | Not confident. |
| No.8 | Moody irresponsible |
| No.9 | Underachiever. |
| No.10 | Self-defeating fears and Anxieties. |

However, the investigator felt that in the next and in the final phase of the intervention program she would be able to solve those problems which the students were facing only if :-

1. The student felt very good about what they did in the group.
2. Had enough trust in the investigator and appreciate that she had provided a caring place for them.
3. Believed the work which the investigator would assign was always useful.
4. Were willing to put a great deal of effort into what they do.

But even if the investigator was able to incorporate these four working conditions into her exercises, she did not expect improvement in the student's behaviour immediately, because very few students had though about shading their problems in the above mentioned ways, and nearly most of the students making effort to get rid of their problems for the first time in their lives.

Therefore the investigator's main job was to persuade them, to continue her effort until the students experienced the joy of getting improvement. But that need a lot of patience on the investigator's part.

However the exercises in the following phase were given to the students either individually or in small group or to the whole group.

However the investigator made a chart for herself for
properly encouraging absence of the problematic behavior.

4.20     <u>Summary of steps</u>

   1.  Identify need
   2.  Set long term goal
   3.  Plan basis of reinforcement
   4.  Decide length of initial sessions
   5.  Set short term objectives
   6.  Plan settings
   7.  Plan triggers
   8.  Plan results
   9.  Prepare supportive materials
  10.  Plan record of progress
  11.  Write programme
  12.  Implement review & move on.

## III Phase

### 4.21 Relearning :

The last and the most important phase of this programme is Relearning. Actually no definite change in the programme occurs in this phase. Relearning was merged into the whole treatment. However, in this phase, student would learn effective ways of behavior. With his newly acquired responsible behavior, he begins to fulfill his needs, finds new relationship, more satisfying involvements, and need others' help less and less. In the Relearning period following exercises had been provided by the investigator to make the students a better citizen in the true sense of the term various group activities were given to the students in this final phase.

In this phase the investigator helped the students to increase group cohesion, sense of responsibility, educational aspiration, achievement motivation, right attitude toward school, proper study, habit, developing sense of belongingness and to build up self-esteem and assertiveness.

### 4.22    Session No.1 -  Group Cohesion :

#### Objective :

To increase the group cohesion among group members, through various group activities which provide opportunity for. creative activity, develop a sense of belongingness and to understand the importance of cooperative efforts.

#### Procedure:

The various group activities which were introduced by the investigator as follow :-

a) Frequent changes in sitting arrangement - It had its impact on the behavior of the pupil. Toward the end of the intervention programme the isolated pupil mixed with other pupil of the group. The students thus got confidence in themselves and started taking initiative in the group activities.

b) Competition - In the group, students were again divided into sub-groups. The members of the sub-group worked together for school subjects. The competitive spirit was aroused in them for concern for excellence. However, the investigator was very careful about the healthy atmosphere of the group.

Both academic and non-academic items were included in the group work, such as preparing charts on the school subjects, project works, spelling games, collection of study materials and various such other things.

Debriefing :

The session was followed by students sharing their own experiences.

4.23 Session -2 : Leisure time and constructive use of it

Objective :

The purpose of this session is to help the students to decide how to get the very most out of their unscheduled time.

Procedure :

The investigator encouraged the students to explore new uses for their unscheduled time in keeping with their interests and curiosity. She also encouraged the students to make some specific plans and to return to the following meeting prepared to discuss what they observed regarding their own use of time and that of others as well as how well their own plans worked out.

To facilitate the process she then distributed some questionnaire to the students.

a) What activities you do before and after school hours.

b) Why do you like to do those activities. You may write some reasons.

c) Are your activities beneficial to you ? Have you experienced any advantage ? What is it ?

d) How could you use your leisure time for better satisfaction.

The investigator provided encouragement to the students by being continually optimistic enthusiastic and positive about the students, learning to be in better control of their use of time and gaining from using the time effectively.

Debriefing :

The session was followed by students sharing their own experiences.

4.24        Session - 3 :    Self-evaluation

Objective :

   To help the students to evaluate their own works and to
improve it.

Procedure :

   The investigator made effort to teach the students how to
evaluate their own works and then asked them to do the evaluation by themselves.  The investigator sent out a constant
message to the students that almost all work could be improved.
Even if the initial work was judged as quality, students were
encouraged by the investigator to see if a little additional
effort would result in improvement.  The investigator stressed
the point that quality takes precedence over quantity.  A large
volume of low quality work has nothing to do with anything of
value.  She also added that there is no better human feeling
than that which comes from the satisfaction of doing something
useful that one believe is the very best one can do, and finding
that others agree.

   Each student was then suggested to make a diagram as
under and to proceed.

contd.

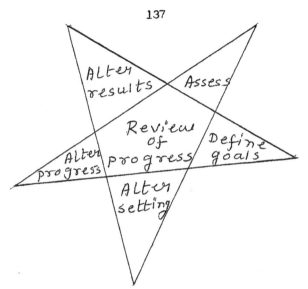

Table : 1 - Responding to the problematic behavior

Debriefing :

The session was followed by students sharing their own experiences.

4.25     Session - 4:   The educational aspiration boosting
                        programme :

Objective :

To help the students to develop their aspiration for education.

Procedure :

Four tests were given to the group students. These tests were objective cum short essay type. The results of the tests were feed back to the students alongwith a descriptive evaluation of each obtained results. After each feedback the student set a goal for themselves on a specified proforma.

Table No.2

Name :
Class:
School :

Subjects : 1.
2.
3.

| Group Test held on | Subject | Student's actual score | Group's average score | Goal set by the student for the next test | Investigator's comment | Guardian's comment on the student's performance |
|---|---|---|---|---|---|---|
| 1 | 2 | 3 | 4 | 5 | 6 | 7 |

Each time the students took a test thus had before them the scores they obtained in the previous tests and the goal they set for themselves for the forthcoming test. Each goal was set on the basis of the knowledge of their latest performance.

Debriefing :

    The session was followed by students sharing their own experiences.

4.26      Session - 5  Development of Academic Skill

Objective :

    To help the students to develop their skill in Academics.

Procedure :

    This special session covered listening attentively, taking notes, concentrating in the class, scheduling time and goals, preparing for and taking examinations, conquering examinations and other anxieties and individually selecting self-improvement projects.  An effective study behavior schedule was made with the help of the students.

Effective study behavior schedule :

I.   General study behavior :

   A)   Proper setting :

   1.   Place : Having a location which is conducive to concentration which is free from auditory and visual distraction and which provides optimal comfort (that is proper lighting, ventilation and temperature but not so relaxing that drowsiness results)

   2.   Time : Schedule yourself - so that class time + study time totals not more than 10 hours a day.

Work efficiently – try for 60-90 minutes of concentrated study of a time, then take a short break. Try to predict the amount of time you should be taking for certain tasks (this probably will vary for your different subjects)

(B)  Proper strategy :

1.  Use a study schedule.
2.  Assignment procedure.

a)  Record assignments in a book. Have a clear conception of what is required and for when it must be completed. If you are not sure ask questions from your teachers.

b)  Gather necessary materials. Use all available resources. Ask teachers for assistance in locating the most appropriate materials.

c)  Do your most difficult assignments during your best concentration periods. Save your rewriting tasks for periods when your concentration are not so good. Try simpler assignments first, therefore building up your confidence.

d)  For essay writing, make a rough outline first, use large blocks of time when you begin to write. Write quickly for the rough draft. Put it aside for 24 hours, then rewrite it. Have someone else read your essay and discuss their comments. Leave essay for another 48 hours, then prepare final draft.

e)  Hand in your assignment on time, everytime.

3.  Study procedure :

    a)  Schedule definite time and outline specific goals
        for your study time. Allow atleast two hours for
        every subject each week for a review of notes and
        text content.

    b)  Question - Ask questions about what should be learned
        during that study time.

    c)  Read - Read the material, Note important items of
        information. Look for answers to the question you
        posed. Realize that scanning is sufficient in
        certain areas while in other places you may need to
        read more analytically.

    d)  Recite - Go over the content which you want to
        remember prepare notes on it in order to help your
        memory.

    e)  Review - Ask further questions and then resurvey the
        material.

II. Specialized Study Behaviour :

    (A) Interactive participation in class.

        1)  Ask the teacher question when clarification of
            lecture points are needed.

        2)  Volunteer answers to questions posed by the
            teachers in the class.

        3)  Participate in class discussion.

142

(B)  Interactive participation out of class.

  1) Engage in formal or informal discussion with class-
     mates on topic relevant to your courses. Clarify
     points which had not been clear during lectures.
     Review course content with other students.

  2) Interact with other resource persons on the
     school campus or in the community.


(C)  Note taking behaviour :

  1) Perview the lecture topic before you go to class.

  2) Read last few day's notes before the class begins.

  3) Listen first, write second.

  4) Use the margins of your paper for headings, write
     lecture content in the body of the page.

  5) Write neatly.
  6) Make special notes of content which the instructor
     stresses.


(D)  Examination Behaviour :

  1) Start preparation early, follow "study procedures"
     mentioned above.
  2) Make notes of instructor's hints concerning
     examination content or format.
  3) Discusse with classmates the areas of course
     which they think are most relevant for the
     examination.
  4) Prepare sample test questions while you study.
     Administer to yourself the day before the
     examination and correct your responses.

(E)  Self observation :

This technique encouraged the student to observe himself objectively. The actual recording equipment
was a simple 3x5 inch card on which the student make
a check mark everytime he completed a study assignment. Regardless of the equipment the data had one
purpose. They were gathered as a baseline against
which to evaluate change in study behaviours

Table No.3

A sample report of self-observation

Name :
Class:

| Day | Date | Subject | Number of assignments done | Time spent |
|-----|------|---------|---------------------------|------------|
| 1 | 2 | 3 | 4 | 5 |

Debriefing :

Without any particular instruction in the class, students who charted their rates generally began to make increases. For some students those increases were in steps with sudden sparts and then Plateasues, followed by further spurts. Other students showed steady increase over several weeks.


4.27        Session No.6    Stimulus control

Objective :

The objective was to plan more effective study strategies and to help the students to take personal responsibilities for their academics and the actions which are related to academics.

Procedure :

One of the most difficult problem of students seemed to be developing adequate concentration while studying. Students reported that their minds wander particularly when they were studying topics that they did not enjoy. As a part of the improvement of-concentration students were educated to see that concentration could be a habit. Students were given explicit formal instruction in the techniques of behavioural self-control. They learnt a bit about the psychology of reward and punishment, contracting and shaping their study habits. Then they were asked to apply these techniques to themselves. They chose aspects of their own behaviour to observe and modify, selected the contingencies and they applied the pay offs to themselves.

Debriefing :

Of course not all students were hooked on this technique.
Some were not aware that they had any behavior that they
wished to change. Others thought that formal programmes of
self-control were childish games. The investigator had a very
important role in getting students committed. A certain amount
of modeling and enthusiasm were definitely called for in order
to improve the students.


4.28    Session No.7 - Group Systematic Desensitization of
                        Test anxiety

Objective :

To help the student to rid themselves of test anxiety.

Procedure :

The investigator told the students that this exercise will
be based on the assumption that anxiety is a learned reaction
to specific events and that it can be unlearned through
appropriate techniques. The investigator then distributed the
following explanation to each student with instructions to read
that carefully.

Introduction to Desensitization Principles :

The following procedure was used to overcome some unusually
strong fear of examination which is called desensitization. The
investigator told the students that, it was developed few
decades ago by a psychologist named Joseph Wolpe. He and a

number of other psychologist had used this method with many
kinds of fears and anxieties and they had reported a high
level of success. This approach was based upon the fact that
it was impossible to be afraid and relaxed at the same time.
For example a student might want to ask a teacher a question
or perhaps criticize something the teacher had said. He
might find however when he started to speak that he experienced
shortness of breath, his heart pounded or his hands perspired
He was unable to make his point. These were anxiety reactions
and didn't occur when the student was relaxed.

Therefore an important part of the method involved teaching you to relax as completely as possible. You might think
that you didnot have to be taught how to relax but the fact
was that most people were frequently unaware of their tensions.
The investigator added that once you had learnt how to relax
the group would develop a list of situation in which the
anxiety occurs. That list would contain different degrees of
anxiety.

For example when a teacher announced an examination would
be given within two weeks you might experience a slight degree
of anxiety, that anxiety however is nothing compared to the
anxiety you experience as you actually pass out the examination
in class. In between those two extremes there were probably
a number of situation that called out varying degrees of
anxiety.

This group working together would put the items on a list
in order from the one that produced the least amount of anxiety
up to the one that produced the most. The list was called a
hierarchy. One of the most interesting aspects of the procedure

was that it tended to generalize to real life situations. Even
though the procedure only required you to imagine yourself in
situations related to fear of examinations, though the fear
would decrease in the actual situation.

Debriefing :

After all the students had indicated that they had understand information, the opportunity was given to raise and
discuss questions that the students might have about desensitization.


4.29    Session No.8 - Training in Muscle Relaxation

Objective :

To help the students to relieve their tension by dint of
training in Muscle Relaxation.

Procedure :

The explanation of the importance of relaxation in
desensitization was given verbally by the investigator.
Following an opportunity to raise questions about the relaxation process, group members were instructed to settle themselves as comfortably as possible in their chairs.

The room was darkened. Outside noise was reduced to the
extent possible and students were instructed to remove
glasses watches and anything else that might interfere with
relaxation.

In order to train students in muscle relaxation, the
investigator used the instruction for muscle relaxation which
was made by Robert A. Osterhome. In that instruction the
students alternatively tensed and relaxed twenty-one different
muscle groups. Through‍ the exercises the students were urged
to become aware of the difference between feelings of muscular
tension and feelings of muscle relaxation.

## Debriefing :

Following the conclusion of the exercise students were
given the opportunity to share their reactions to the relaxation
training with one another and with the investigator. The
students wre also given a copy of the following guide for
training in Muscle Relaxation in order to help them practice
relaxation exercise at home.

The guide for training in Muscle Relaxation Instruction
can be found in the Appendix.

## 4.30     Session No.9 -   Test-Anxiety Hierarchy

## Objective :

To help the students to arrange the anxiety provoking
situations in hierarchical order.

## Procedure :

Each students were given a printed copy. The investigator then told the students that below were 15 items which
tend to elicit varying degrees of anxiety. You were to rank
those items from least to most anxiety provoking for you.

In the space before each item place a number corresponding to the degree of anxiety you normally feel when you encounter it. The investigator also added that number 15 would be the item which elicits the most anxiety provoking situation.

- You're sitting in your class and the instructor announces that you will have an examination during the next class session. You wonder if you can prepare in time. There is so much material to be covered.

- It is the day before an important examination, you talk to some of your classmates who tell you how much preparation they have done for this examination. You have spent far less time on the average.

- You are sitting for an important examination to be given the next day. Your grade in this course will probably depend upon your performance on this examination. You are wondering how you will remember the information on the test.

- It is late evening before an important examination. You are tired and having trouble concentrating, but you do not feel really prepared.

- You are in bed the night before an important examination which will determine your final grade. Your mind flashes to the examination.

- You wake up and realize that you have an examination today which will determine your final grade.

- You have an hour of study time left before you will take a very important examination. As you look over your notes you realized that you have become confused. You wonder whether you should continue reviewing your notes or just put them a side.

- You are walking to an important examination which will probably determine your final grade.

- As you enter your classroom the day of an examination, you hear several students discussing possible questions. You realize that you probably could not answer these questions if they were asked on the test.

- You are sitting in your class, waiting for your examination to be passed out. You receive your examination paper. You look at the first question and can't recall the answer.

- As you read over your examination paper, you realize that many of the items are very difficult. You look up from your test, wondering where to start and notice the students around you are writing furiously.

- Many questions on this examination is hazy to you. You realize that you must have skipped over some important facts in your study.

- On this extremely important examination you find that. You have spent too much time on the first portion of the test and must hurry up a bit in order to finish on time.

- With five minutes left on this examination which will probably determine your final grade you see that you left a number of items blank.

Debriefing :

Following the ranking of hierarchy items the students were encouraged to *share* their reactions to their practice in muscle relaxation in the previous week. An attempt was made to resolve any difficulties that a student may have had in the practice sessions and to answer questions about muscle relaxation. (which could be found in the Appendix)

The relaxation technique referred to earlier was thus used again in order to train group numbers even more thoroughly in relaxation. At the completion of the relaxation exercise the students were given training in visualizing neutral scenes.

The students were urged to continue their relaxed state and to attempt to project themselves into the situation, so that they could gain practice in imagning themselves in real life situations.


4.31    Session No.10    Working Through the Hierarchy items.

Objective :

To help the students to work through the hierarchy items.

Procedure :

The last session of the treatment program was devoted to working through the individual items of the test-anxiety hierarchy. The first fifteen minutes of each session were used to induce a deep state of relaxation among the students. The remaining 45 minutes were used to work through four or five items on the hierarchy.

As the group members have had two previous experiences
with the recorded relaxation instructions and had practiced
relaxation procedures at home for two weeks, the investigator
found that most can be relaxed in approximately fifteen minutes
during the third session.

Afetr the relaxation instructions, the investigator
announced that with in a few minutes the students would have
read to them a description of the scene that they had ranked
at the previous session as the least anxiety provoking. The
students were told that if they experience anxiety in themselves,
they could tell that to the investigator by simply raising
the index finger of either hand. The students were also
urged to try to project themselves as completely as possible
into the description of the hierarchy item.

After each presentation of a hierarchy item students
were given 15 to 20 seconds of relaxation instruction (For
example - let your arms relax. Take a deep breath and hold
it - now feel the enjoyment as you relax completely) When all
of the presentations of a hierarchy items had been completed,
students were given approximately one minute of relaxation
instructions before the initial presentation of the next
hierarchy item was made.

A Typical Outline for the final sessions look something
like this :

### Session : I

1. Collection of relaxation practice forms from students.
2. Fifteen minutes of relaxation instructions by the
   investigator.

3. Explanation of signaling of anxiety and projecting self into situations, assurance of individual help if anxiety was still signaled following final presentation.

4. Two minutes of relaxation instructions.

5. Presentation of items, from the hierarchy three to five presentation interspersed with 15 to 20 second of relaxation instructions.

6. One minutes of relaxation instructions.

7. Continuation with hierarchy items 2-5 as shown in 5 and 6 above.

## Session : II

1. 15 minutes of relaxation instructions.
2. One or two presentations of hierarchy items 1-5.
3. Presentation of hierarchy items, 6-9.

## Session : III

1. 15 minutes of relaxation instructions.
2. One or two presentations of hierarchy items 1-9.
3. Presentation of hierarchy items 10-12.

## Session : IV

1. 15 minutes of relaxation instructions.
2. One or two presentation of hierarchy items 1-12.
3. Presentation of hierarchy items 13-15.

Debriefing :

The session was followed by students sharing their own experiences. It has been found by the investigator that there was a consistent tendency for the students to report greater reductions in test anxiety.

4.32    Session No.11 :  Development of Problem Solving skill

Objective :

To help the students to develop the problem solving skill.

Procedure :

The investigator introduced the students the skill of solving real life problems. She taught them that the core of problem solving is to learn to use information in a logical way and that the only real purpose of gathering information is to use it.

The following steps of problems solving skill was given by the investigator to the students.

Steps of Problem Solving :

1.    Agreeing to work on the problem.

2.    Choosing one part of the problem to work on.  There may be several different parts of this topic which one would like to work on.  Select one now for discussion and decision making.  The investigator told the students that they may deal with any other parts later select a part that they think is important enough to work on and small a enough to make a decision.

3. Listing possible solutions - List as many possible solutions or suggested actions or plans as you can which you think could solve the problem or help in solving the part you've chosen to work on.

   The investigator told the students in this step each of you simply tries to suggest as many actions or solutions as you can without commenting on them or evaluating them.

. 4. Selecting the appropriate solution - select those actions which you think best for addressing the parts of the problem chosen to work on in step - 2.

5. Deciding action - plan the detailed action you will need to carry out the alternatives just selected. Decide what is to be done, who will do it when it will be done and how. The aim of this step is to clearly specify all of the actions needed to carry out the alternatives agreed to, so that if necessary you could each carry out your decision satisfactorily.

Debriefing :

In this session each of the students solved three of their personal problems which arise either in school or at home. The problems which they are facing have already been pinpointed by themselves by the investigator in the previous phase.

4.33    Session No.12 : Fostering interest for Achievement
                        Motivation

Objective :

To help the students to get interested in achievement
motivation and thus to increase self-esteem.

Procedure :

The investigator told the students to write down the
answer of the following  questions.

(a)    List and describe four of your tasks of the past
       two years and of the present that you consider
       most important.

       1st task        _____
       2nd task        _____
       3rd task        _____
       4th task        _____

How would you describe your chances of success for the
various tasks you have _____

(a)    Successful if you pay attention and don't to some-
       thing foolish.
(b)    Successful but only if you work hard and think
       constantly of new ways of doing things.
(c)    Successful but only if you're lucky.

What is the best position you expect to attain in your
school life _____

How much thought have you given to it within the past
years none _____

a little _____
fair amount _____
a great deal _____

Looking back over the past two years do you feel that
you've made very good progress toward  your goal _____?
-    good progress toward your goal _____?
-    No progress toward your goal  _____?

When you compare yourself with people about your age and
educational background.

Do you feel you have been less successful in your work
than they have been _____

About as successful in your work than they have been_____

More successful in your work than they have been _____

Describe the most important ways in which you have
changed in the past two years _____

Debriefing :

     The session was followed by students sharing their own
experiences.

4.34    Session No.13  Developing sense of Responsibility
                       among the students

Objective :

   To help the students to develop sense of responsibility.

Procedure :

   The investigator introduced the topic in a general way.
She then posed two questions to the group.

   (a)  What do you mean by the sense of responsibility.

   (b)  Name some such persons from our contemporary life
        who have shown a great sense of responsibility
        under difficult conditions.

   A practical problem connected with a N.C.C. Camp was then
proposed.  The class then discussed the various tasks and
responsibilities needed to conduct the camp successfully.

   The investigator summed up by calling attention to the
importance of team work in discharging responsibilities for
the success of any such work.

Teaching Responsibility through students commitment :

   The basic tenet of this program is that students must
learn to take greater responsibility for their immediate
educational future.  In the  course the student was asked to
make a commitment to objectives toward which he would work
during the semester.

The student was allowed only a contract for an average
or above average grade on the ground that anything less does
not represent an appropriate return to him from the course.
What constitute the required performance for each grade level
was pre-set by the student himself. The accepted course was
divided into units. Each unit in turn consisted of several
learning activities. Each activity required the student to
demonstrate that he had reached the performance level.
Considerable work was done in preparation for the student's
decision making concerning the commitments he would make.
The students write goals, describing their objectives for the
course.

Being the decision maker concerning what these objectives would be and how he would work toward them created a
responsibility on the part of the student to live up to the
terms of his decisions. The investigator counseled with the
student to help him select objectives and establish work
patterns.

The student worked to accomplish these objectives and
the investigator was available as tutor and resource person.
Each assignment submitted by the student was evaluated by the
investigator on a pass or incomplete scale according to
whether the students work had met the objectives of that
activity. The student was given ample opportunity to master
the learning activity rather than being penalized for failing
to meet the criteria.

The investigator counseled with the student to help him
see where and how he needs to work to improve his performance.
The investigator tried to encourage students to work consistent
to accomplish their commitments.

However the investigator did not give into below level
performance but instead returned such work to the student
with offer of assistance and encouragement.

Debriefing :

The session was followed by students sharing their own
experiences.

4.35      Session No.14   Assertiveness Training

Objective :

To develop sense of assertiveness among students.

Procedure :

In this phase exercises were given to the students  to
increase their assertive behaviour. Initially the students
received a rationale for Assertiveness Training from the
investigator. The rationale was as follow - "We are convinced
that being assertive is a skill that one can learn. Developing behaviour skills it is essential to research or practice
elements of that skill. The investigator added that people
can rehearse situations in their imagination. Imagining
certain selected situation can alter one's behaviour in those
actual situation. The investigator also added that the
procedure we were using was based on imagination practice and
learning. She told to the students "I'll describe a scene to
you and you have to imagine it.

The investigator selected different students for different scenes and while one particular student was playing the
role, the other students were observing it.

During the series of role enactments one students (the
model) was instructed to maintain eye contact with another
student to whom he was delivering his response.

When an acceptable level of eye contact was established
instructions for the first student to talk in a louder more
forceful tone of voice were given. After a stable pattern
of increased eye contact and vocal aptitude had been achieved
the first student (the model) was instructed to talk long
enough to the other student, so that the second student
would fully understand his position. At that point instructions alone proved to be ineffective, for the student lacked
sufficient verbal skills to put his point across. Therefore
in this phase of training the investigator modeled some
replies appropriate to each situation. During subsequent
rehearsals the investigator continued modeling and gave feedback and the role playing student modeled responses with
which he felt most comfortable. When duration of appropriate
speech reached an appropriate level as judged by the investigator, the investigator then modeled increased assertiveness
by further modifying content. The following exercises were
given to the group.

(a) Picture yourself at a concert with a friend. A few
people in the row behind you are making a lot of
noise and disturbing everyone. It seems they have
a comment to make every few minutes which everyone
can hear. A person sitting next to you (the model)
turns around and say "will you people please be
quite".

(b)    Imagine the person (model) is staying at a hotel.
After one night there he/she noticed that the bed
springs was broken. The bed sags miserably and was
very uncomfortable during the night. In the morn-
ing the person went to the clerk of the desk and
said - "The bed in my room is quite uncomfortable.
I believe it is broken, I wish you would replace
the bed or change my room."

(c)    Picture yourself in a department store waiting at
a counter for a salesperson. In the store the
person (model) was returning a thing that he/she
recently received from the shop. The sales person
claimed that the store could not give back cash
for returned merchandise. The person claimed
"there is nothing I see that I use it. Since it
is hard for me to get back money in the case of a
faulty merchandise, it is unlikely I'll ever shop
here again. I think if at all possible you should give
a cash refund."

(d)    Imagine the person (model) in his/her apartment
around dinner time. The person had an important
appointment later in the evening but friends dropped
in for a visit. The person was getting somewhat
bothered about the appointment and had to leave in
a few minutes. While the friends were sitting
there and every one was chatting the person broke
into the conversation and said I'm really glad that
you dropped in but I have a meeting and have to
leave. Perhaps we can get together sometime when
we are both free.

However, at the end of each treatment session the investigator routinely administered a questionnaire to find out whether the student had any difficulty or feeling anxious in imagining the scenes and in playing the role.

4.36    Session No.15 :    Developing the thought of success
                            among students

Objective :

To stimulate and promote thoughts of success among students.

Procedure :

The investigator in this programme helped to strengthen the desire to succeed and tried to creat a readiness to under-take work for their goals. Discussion, Question and answers, small group work,essay writing and mental exercises, formed the methods of work. The investigator started by recalling the various qualities of a successful person. She then asked the students to recall some successful events from their lives. She told the students, to write about those events and share those events in the group. She then summed up by saying that for success qualities like goal setting, sacrifice, self-confidence, hard work and a keen desire to succeed are needed. She also added that thoughts of success are necessary for real success. She emphasized the point that persons who think they would succeed and who works hard to get this success are more likely to succeed.

Debriefing :

The session was followed by students sharing their own experiences.

## 4.37    Session No.16 : Life goal

### Objective :

To help the students to learn how to choose life goal rather than what to choose and to provide specific facts for his immediate choice.

### Procedure :

This exercise was last of all exercises of the final phase. Here the investigator gave some instructions to the students so that the students could have complete image about their life goal. Same type of questionnaire of defining goals and the barriers also were given previously. But here at the end of programme the investigator wanted to have a total picture of the effect of intervention program on the student and how did it affect their thinking on defining and setting goals and how to deal with the barriers effectively.

The investigator felt that before the student was ready to make decision seriously, he must be assured that specific long range goals need not be set before he could deal with immediate choices. Most ninth graders had been continually asked by parents, teachers and other adults about what they want to do in life. Since they were not ready to answer this question, they often had the notion that until they knew for sure where they were headed, they were just marking time. Some were discouraged about looking ahead at all because they thought everyone else really knew where he was going except him/her. It was helpful first to let students discuss their own plans and feelings about the future.

The investigator started by saying "Dear students, soon
you will be planning your high school programme. The story
of what happened to students like you was part of the information, you need to know at this time. I am giving you a
questionnaire. I will not question what you choose, I'll
only help you to learn how to choose." Then, the students
completed a planned questionnaire as under.

Take a sheet of paper, draw a line that represents your
life, past, present & future.

Think of your life once again considering yourself, your
attitudes, abilities, strengths and weaknesses etc. You may
depict yourself as of today in the form of any figure.

List down four/five important goals you have in life.
Subsequently rank them in the order of priority.

Choose one or two from among the most important goals.
Write goals for the next six months. These short term goals
should be such that they relate to the one/two important long
term goals.

Then the investigator asked the participants to estimate
the probability of success in achieving each of the short
term goals. They indicated their expectations in percentage,
100% sure, 60% probably etc. Then they worked out detailed
outline of activities that would be needed to undertake in
order to achieve the short term goals and listed them down
with a time frame.

Then the students anticipated the obstacles that he/she
was likely to face in achieving each of the short term goals:
and wrote Roadlocks in two categories -

a)   Personal
b)   Environmental.

and identified the help that he/she would like to initiate in
order to overcome these blocks.

Then the investigator asked the students -
How would you feel if you fail to achieve that goal ?   and
How would you feel if you succeed ?

The result of that questionnaire provided the group with
their first group discussion on each of their life goal. The
group found that at least 3 out of 10 students had no idea at
all of what they wanted to do in future.  Another 4 out of
10 had a vague idea and only a few students were certain
about their long range goals.

The investigator pointed out that many senior students
in college had no more idea of what they wanted to do than
the present ninth graders today.  She then gave a short
lecture on the necessity of being realistic about goals.  She
then told the students that decisions about the future
requires a different approach.

Students were then informed of these pre-requisites to
good decision making -

They are :-

1) Specific facts about ·the choice.
2) A knowledge of other available alternatives.
3) Some estimation of the possible consequences.

Others factors such as risk-taking and strategy were also involved.

The investigator then helped the students to make a realistic decision in which the student had a likely chance of success. In the final analysis, this was judged by the student himself. When the students were given specific information about choices that were judged by the investigator to be more comensurate with their abilities.

## Debriefing :

The session was followed by students sharing their own experiences.

## EVALUATION

## Parent Reaction :

Ninth grade students were reluctant to discuss their high school plans with parents. But the investigator again and again urged the students to share their experience with their families. The result was most parents were enthusiastic in their response, they seemed grateful and relieved to receive such data about future goal alternatives and consequences about their wards.

Student Reaction :

The intervention programme was ended by the evaluation
of the programme by the student themselves, and they filled
the following questionnaire to reflect their exact ideas about
the programme.

a)   The things which I have learned from this programme
     and which have enriched me _____

b)   The things which I have discovered about myself
     from the programme which was not aware of
     before _____

c)   Some special experiences in the course which  I'll
     remember _____

Then each individual student wrote few lines on -

-   My impression about the programme _____
-   My impression about the group        _____
-   My impression about the
    programme director                   _____

Having discussed at length the development of Reality
Therapy training package for students, organization of the
training programme and conduction at the experiment, the next
step is to analyze the available data both qualitatively and
quantitatively in order to find out the significance of the
programme for students.

169

CHAPTER : V

DATA ANALYSES

5.0 Introduction :

As stated in chapter IV an intervention programme based
on Reality Therapy had been developed and tried out on 30
students of class IX of Baroda city during 1993-94 academic
session. The difference in the performance of students on
the dependent variable measured before and after the intervention was the criterion for judging the effectiveness of
the Reality Therapy approach adopted. However, the effectiveness of the intervention programme had been studied both
quantitatively and qualitatively. Data were collected on
each of the variables using the tools and the procedures
outlined in Chapter III. The collected data were analyzed
separately for each variable. Detailed description of the
analysis of data and the inferences drawn in respect of the
stated objectives of the study are presented in the sections
to follow.

5.1 Assertiveness :

It refers to the ability to stand for one-self, one's
right and constructively communicate one's need as well as
to take care of one's need. It is a state when one does not
feel being a victim nor does one victimize others.

Here, students' assertiveness had been measured through
Tasneem Naqvi's Assertiveness Scale. The Means, standard
deviations of the Assertiveness Scale on the six observations
were presented in Table (1), Table (2) and Table (3) respectively.

However, the arrangement of the quantitative data of the three schools were as follows :

a)   Baroda High School
b)   M. G. M. School
c)   Rosary School.

## Table No.1

### Baroda High School

Means, standard deviations of Assertiveness Scale on the six observations

| Observation | Mean | Standard deviation |
|---|---|---|
| 01 | 3.6 | 1.11 |
| 02 | 3.6 | 1.11 |
| 03 | 3.6 | 1.20 |
| Intervention . . . . . . . . . . . . . . . . . . . . . . |  |  |
| 04 | 5.3 | 0.90 |
| 05 | 5.4 | 1.02 |
| 06 | 5.8 | 1.17 |

Table No.2

M. G. M. School

Means, standard deviations of Assertiveness Scale
on the six observations

| Observation | Mean | Standard Deviation |
|---|---|---|
| 01 | 3.0 | 0.89 |
| 02 | 2.8 | 0.60 |
| 03 | 2.9 | 0.54 |
| Intervention . . . . . . . . . . . . . . . . . . . . . | | |
| 04 | 4.6 | 0.66 |
| 05 | 4.6 | 0.66 |
| 06 | 4.6 | 0.49 |

Table No.3

Rosary School

Means, standard deviations of Assertiveness Scale
on the six observations

| Observation | Mean | Standard Deviation |
|---|---|---|
| 01 | 2.8 | 0.75 |
| 02 | 3.1 | 0.54 |
| 03 | 2.9 | 0.70 |
| Intervention . . . . . . . . . . . . . . . . . . . . . | | |
| 04 | 3.7 | 0.64 |
| 05 | 3.8 | 0.75 |
| 06 | 4.1 | 1.14 |

From Table No.1,2 and 3 it was clear that the mean scores
steadily increased in all the three schools in the post-
intervention phase while there was a mild difference among
means in the pre-intervention phase. This might indicate that
the students' sense of assertiveness was affected positively
by the intervention though there was difference in degree of
improvement among the schools.

The data were further subjected to 't' test analyses to
determine the level of the significance of the differences
between means of the six observations of the three schools.
Presented in table (4) (5) and (6) were the calculated 't'
values between the various possible pairs of observations.
Table (4) (5) and (6) showed that the means of the pre-
intervention observations differed significantly with the
means of the post-intervention observations.

## Table No.4

### Baroda High School

| Observation | I | II | III | IV | V | VI |
|---|---|---|---|---|---|---|
| \multicolumn{7}{l}{'t' values of means of scores on Assertiveness Scale on various possible pairs of observatins} |
| I | - | - | - | - | - | - |
| II | - | - | - | - | - | - |
| III | - | - | - | - | - | - |
| IV | 6.53** | 7.08** | 4.27** | - | - | - |
| V | 6.92** | 6.92** | 4.54** | 2.56 | - | - |
| VI | 7.33** | 10.00** | 4.00** | 2.00 | 2.00 | - |

df = 9

\* = significant at 0.05 level
\*\* = significant at 0.01 level

BARODA HIGH SCHOOL

Means of scores of Assertiveness
plotted against the six observations

Means of Scores

Observations

Means of scores of Assertiveness
plotted against the six observations

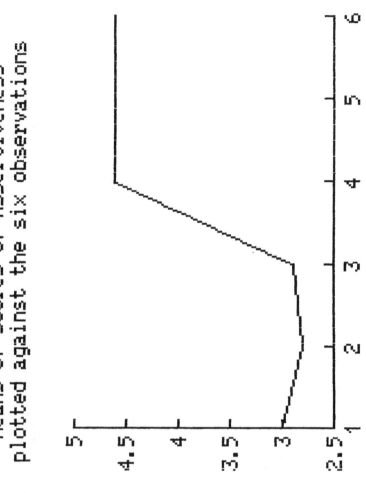

Means of Scores

Observations

Means of scores of Assertiveness
plotted against the six observations

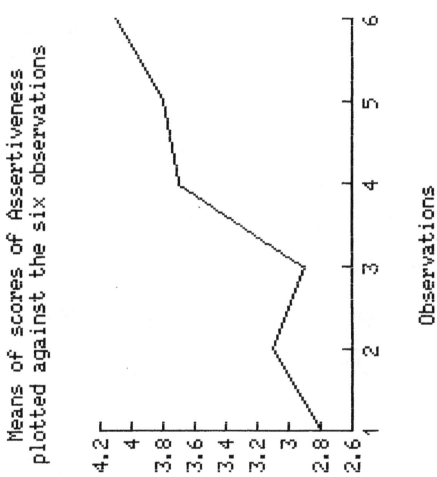

Means of Scores

Observations

## Table No.5

### M.G.M. School

't' values of means of scores on Assertiveness Scale on various possible pairs of observations

| Observations | I | II | III | IV | V | VI |
|---|---|---|---|---|---|---|
| I | - | - | - | - | - | - |
| II | 0.57 | - | - | - | - | - |
| III | 0.26 | 0.43 | - | - | - | - |
| IV | 0.71** | 7.05** | 6.53** | - | - | - |
| V | 5.71** | 6.42** | 7.08** | - | - | - |
| VI | 10.05** | 7.05** | 8.00** | - | - | - |

df = 9

\* = significant at 0.05 level
\*\* = significant at 0.01 level

## Table No.6

### Rosary School

't' values of means of scores on Assertiveness Scale on various possible pairs of observations.

| Observation | I | II | III | IV | V | VI |
|---|---|---|---|---|---|---|
| I | - | - | - | - | - | - |
| II | 2.05 | - | - | - | - | - |
| III | 0.37 | 0.34 | - | - | - | - |
| IV | 2.64** | 2.05 | 2.68** | - | - | - |
| V | 0.125 | 2.59 | 1.12 | - | - | - |
| VI | 2.07 | 2.56** | 2.92** | 0.12 | 0.13 | - |

df = 9

\* = significant at 0.05 level
\* = sigbificant at 0.01 level

The results could be better appreciated if one took a
look at the graphical representation  Plotted on Graph (1)(2)
and (3) were the means of the percentages of the Assertiveness scores on the six observations. One could easily observe
that the rate of increase was greater in the post-intervention
phase. This indicated that Reality Therapy did affect
positively the sense of assertiveness of the students.


## 5.2 Responsibility :

Responsibility is the ability to fulfill one's needs. A
responsible person also does that which gives him a feeling
of self-worth and a feeling that he is worthwhile to others.
Students' sense of responsibility  had been measured through
a Responsibility Scale prepared by the investigator.

The Means and the standard Deviations of the Responsibility Scale on the six observations were presented in table
(7)  (8)  and (9).

From the tables it appeared that there was a considerable
increase in the Mean Scores in the post-intervention phase.
The data were further subjected to 't' tests to determine the
level of significance of the difference between Means of the
six observations of the sample students of the three schools.
The 't' test analyses were presented in Table (10)  (11)  and
(12) which showed that there was significant difference
between means of the pre-intervention phase and the means of
the post intervention phase on Responsibility dimension.

Table No.7    Baroda High School

Means, standard Deviations of the Responsibility
Scale on the six observations

| Observation | Mean | Standard Deviation |
|---|---|---|
| 01 | - | - |
| 02 | 2.6 | 0.49 |
| 03 | 2.6 | 0.65 |
| Intervention . . . . . . . . . . . . . . . . . . . . . . . . | | |
| 04 | 7.4 | 1.69 |
| 05 | 7.6 | 1.43 |
| 06 | 7.7 | 1.55 |

Table No.8    M.G.M. School

Means, standard Deviations of the Responsibility
Scale on the six observations.

| Observation | Mean | Standard Deviation |
|---|---|---|
| 01 | -.7 | - |
| 02 | 3.7 | 0.78 |
| 03 | 3.6 | 0.80 |
| Intervention . . . . . . . . . . . . . . . . . . . . . . . . | | |
| 04 | 6.1 | 1.70 |
| 05 | 6.5 | 1.36 |
| 06 | 6.6 | 1.63 |

Table No.9          Rosary   School

Means, standard Deviations of the Responsibility Scale on
the six observations

| Observation | Mean | Standard Deviation |
|---|---|---|
| 01 | - | - |
| 02 | 2.5 | 0.50 |
| 03 | 2.8 | 0.60 |
| Intervention . . . . . . . . . . . . . . . . . . . . . . | | |
| 04 | 5.3 | 1.10 |
| 05 | 5.8 | 0.98 |
| 06 | 6.1 | 1.04 |

Table No.10
Baroda High School

t-values of means of scores on the sense of responsibility
scale on the various possible pairs of observations

| Observations | I | II | III | IV | V | VI |
|---|---|---|---|---|---|---|
| I | - | - | - | - | - | - |
| II | - | - | - | - | - | - |
| III | - | - | - | - | ᴰᵉ | - |
| IV | - | 8.13** | 8.13** | - | - | - |
| V | - | 9.80** | 8.78** | - | - | - |
| VI | - | 10.02** | 9.10** | - | - | - |

df  =  9
*   =  significant at 0.05 level
** =  significant at 0.01 level.

BAPODA HIGH SCHOOL

Means of scores of sense-responsibility plotted against the five observations

Observations

Means of Scores

Means of scores of sense-responsibility
plotted against the five observations

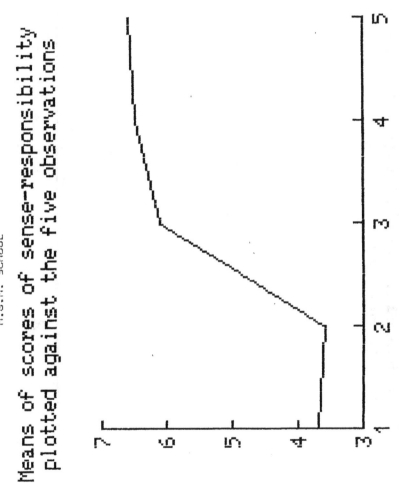

Observations

Means of Scores

Means of scores of sense-responsibility
plotted against the five observations

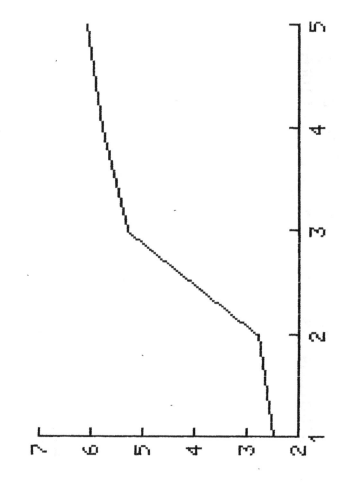

Observations

Means of Scores

## Table No.11

### M.G.M. School

t-values of means of scores on sense of responsibility scale
on various possible pairs of observations

| Observation | I | II | III | IV | V | VI |
|---|---|---|---|---|---|---|
| I | - | - | - | - | - | - |
| II | - | - | - | - | - | - |
| III | - | - | - | - | - . | - |
| IV | - | 4.08** | 4.05** | - | - | - |
| V | - | 6.08** | 5.17** | - | - | - |
| VI | - | 4.83** | 5.08** | - | - | - |

df = 9
\* = significant at 0.05 level
\*\* = significant at 0.01 level

## Table No.12

### Rosary School

t-values of means of scores on Responsibility scale on
various possible pairs of observations.

| Observation | I | II | III | IV | V | VI |
|---|---|---|---|---|---|---|
| I | - | - | - | - | - | - |
| II | - | - | - | - | - | - |
| III | - | 1.03 | - | - | - | , - |
| IV | - | 7.14** | 5.31** | - | - | - |
| V | - | 7.05** | 6.38** | - | - | - |
| VI | - | 9.00** | 7.02** | 1.77 | 0.11 | - |

df = 9
\*+ = significant at 0.05 level
\*\* + significant at 0.01 level

The result could be better appreciated if one took a look at the Graphical Representations. Plotted on Graph (4) (5) and (6) were the means of the percentages of the Responsibility Scores on the six observations. From the graphs one could easily observe that the rate of increase was greater in the post-intervention phase.

From all the above mentioned analyses it appread that the programme of Reality Therapy helped to increase the sense of Responsibility of the students though it differed in degree from school to school due to some unavoidable circumstances.

## 5.3 Attitude toward School :

The attitude toward school refers the way the students had come to feel about their total school experience — how hard they wanted to work in school, how highly they value school and how much they wanted to pursue further schooling.

Students' attitude toward school was measured through school Attitude Measure Inventor of Lawrence J. Dolan & Marci More Enos. Table No. (13) (14) and (15) shows the Means standard Deviations of school Attitude Measure Scale on the six observations and Table No.(16) (17) and (18) shows the 't' values between the means of various possible pairs of observations. Graphs (7) (8) and (9) are the graphical representation of the mean values of each variable of each school.

## Table No.13

### Baroda High School

Means, standard Deviations of Attitude toward school
scale on the six observations

| Observation | Mean | Standard Deviation |
|:---:|:---:|:---:|
| 01 | 28.4 | 5.73 |
| 02 | 28.8 | 3.40 |
| 03 | 28.0 | 2.28 |
| Intervention . . . . . . . . . . . . . . . . . . . . . . . . |  |  |
| 04 | 64.2 | 5.29 |
| 05 | 65.6 | 5.13 |
| 06 | 66.6 | 4.18 |

## Table No.14

### M.G.M. School

Means, standard Deviations of Attitude toward school
scale on the six observations

| Observation | Mean | Standard Deviation |
|:---:|:---:|:---:|
| 01 | 27.1 | 4.08 |
| 02 | 26.4 | 3.96 |
| 03 | 25.9 | 3.18 |
| Intervention . . . . . . . . . . . . . . . . . . . . . . . . |  |  |
| 04 | 51.4 | 8.18 |
| 05 | 52.0 | 7.86 |
| 06 | 49.5 | 8.24 |

## Table No. 15

### Rosary  School

Means, Standard Deviations of Attitude toward school
Scale on the six observations

| Observation | Mean | Standard Deviation |
|---|---|---|
| O1 | 29.2 | 3.99 |
| O2 | 30.4 | 3.72 |
| O3 | 30.5 | 4.48 |
| Intervention . . . . . . . . . . . . . . . . . . . . . . . . . | | |
| O4 | 41.3 | 4.98 |
| O5 | 43.2 | 2.82 |
| O6 | 45.4 | 2.58 |

## Table No. 16

### Baroda High School

t values of means of scores of Attitude toward school scale
on various possible pairs of observations

| Observation | I | II | III | IV | V | VI |
|---|---|---|---|---|---|---|
| I. | - | - | - | - | - | - |
| II. | 0.04 | - | - | - | - | - |
| III. | - | - | - | - | - | - |
| IV. | 18.17** | 18.67** | 19.05** | - | - | - |
| V. | 17.06** | 20.02** | 22.06** | - | - | - |
| VI. | 17.03** | 20.00** | 22.05** | - | - | - |

df = 9

\* = significant at 0.05 level

\*\* = significant at 0.01 level

Means of scores of Attitude to School
plotted against the six observations

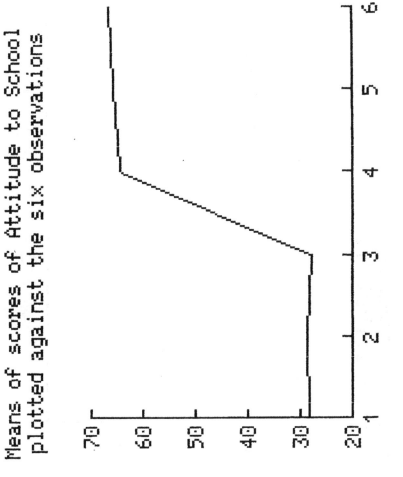

Means of Scores

Observations

M.G.M. SCHOOL

Means of scores of Attitude to School
plotted against the six observations

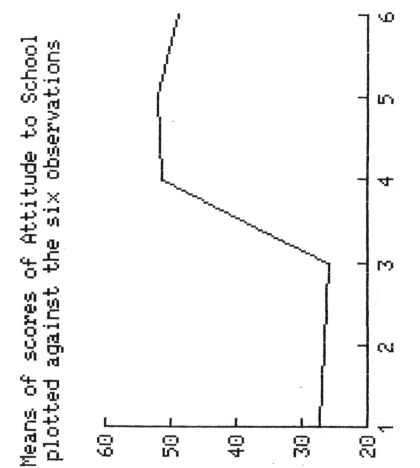

Observations

Means of Scores

Means of scores of Attitude to School
plotted against the six observations

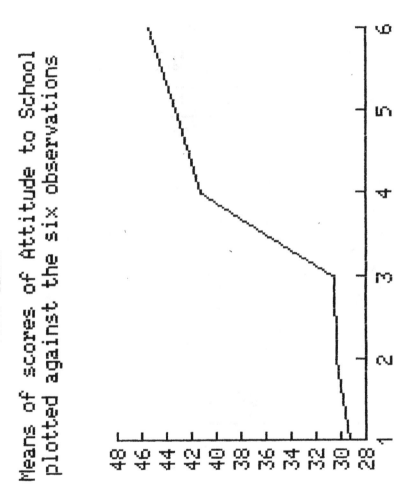

Means of Scores

Observations

181

## Table No.17

### M. G. M. School

t values of means of scores of Attitude toward school scale
on various possible pairs of observations

| Observation | I | II | III | IV | V | VI |
|---|---|---|---|---|---|---|
| I | – | – | – | – | – | – |
| II | – | – | – | – | – | – |
| III | – | – | – | – | – | – |
| IV | 12.85** | 14.36** | 12.81** | – | – | – |
| V | 11.08** | 14.06** | 13.45** | – | – | – |
| VI | 10.56** | 12.48** | 11.07** | – | – | – |

df = 9
\* = significant at 0.05 level
\*\* = significant at 0.01 level

## Table No.18

### Rosary school

t values of means of scores of Attitude toward school scale
on various possible pairs of observations

| Observations | I | II | III | IV | V | VI |
|---|---|---|---|---|---|---|
| I | – | – | – | – | – | – |
| II | 1.92 | – | – | – | – | – |
| III | 1.27 | – | – | – | – | – |
| IV | 5.84** | 6.60** | 7.02** | – | – | – |
| V | 9.21** | 8.64** | 6.64** | – | – | – |
| VI | 12.02** | 10.48** | 11.48** | – | – | – |

df = 9
\* = significant at 0.05 level
\*\* = significant at 0.01 level

However from the post-intervention scores it appear that the scores are towards the higher end of the range indicating that the students have developed right attitude toward school. Looking at the table of means it can be said that in the baseline phase the mean scores hardly differ. But there a clear jump from the pre-intervention phase to the post-intervention phase. From all the 't' tables it can be noticed that the post intervention means are significantly different from the pre-intervention means.

Graphs represent the data in the visual form. The data path shows steady increase in the direction of the hypothesis. It may be concluded from the finding that the significant difference in the means of pre and post-intervention phase may have been due to the effect of the intervention.

## 5.4  Educational Aspiration :

Educational Aspiration is the educational level which an individual wishes to reach. Its role is important in the field of education, as an individual's achievement can't be viewed as successful or unsuccessful unless a statement of his level of aspiration is obtained. Students educational aspiration was measured through Nageswara Rao's Educational Aspiration Scale.

Means, standard Deviations were calculated from the obtained raw scores on the six observations. Table No.19, 20 and 21 summarises the results. One can easily see from tables that there are consistent increase in the means of scores in the post-intervention phase. Table Nos.(22) (23) and (24) presents the calculated 't' values between the means of all possible pairs of the six observations. Graphs (10) (11) and (12) gives a visual representation of the results. The data path shows that the post-intervention data steadily increases. All those data however show that the intervention may have had influence on the educational aspiration of the students.

## Table No.19

### Baroda High School

Means, standard deviations of Educational Aspiration
Scale on the six observations

| Observation | Mean | Standard Deviation |
|---|---|---|
| 01 | 2.8 | 0.75 |
| 02 | 3.1 | 0.70 |
| 03 | 3.1 | 0.70 |
| Intervention . . . . . . . . . . . . . . . . . . . . . . |  |  |
| 04 | 5.3 | 0.90 |
| 05 | 5.6 | 0.92 |
| 06 | 6.3 | 0.90 |

Table No. 20

M. G. M. School

Means, standard Deviations of Educational Aspiration
Scale on the six observations

| Observation | Mean | Standard Deviations |
|---|---|---|
| 01 | 2.8 | 0.60 |
| 02 | 2.8 | 0.60 |
| 03 | 3.0 | 0.89 |
| Intervention . . . . . . . . . . . . . . . . . . . . . . . . | | |
| 04 | 4.2 | 0.75 |
| 05 | 4.6 | 0.80 |
| 06 | 4.7 | 0.64 |

Table No. 21

Rosary School

Means, standard Deviations of the Educational
Aspiration Scale on the six observations

| Observation | Mean | Standard Deviation |
|---|---|---|
| 01 | 2.7 | 0.64 |
| 02 | 2.7 | 0.64 |
| 03 | 3.1 | 0.54 |
| Intervention . . . . . . . . . . . . . . . . . . . . . . . . | | |
| 04 | 4.1 | 0.54 |
| 05 | 4.3 | 0.78 |
| 06 | 4.4 | 0.66 |

Table No.24

Rosary School

't' values of means of scores on Educational Aspiration Scale
on various possible pairs of observations

| Observation | I | II | III | IV | V | VI |
|---|---|---|---|---|---|---|
| I | - | - | - | - | - | - |
| II | - | - | - | - | - | - |
| III | 1.37 | 2.00 | - | - | - | - |
| IV | 6.36** | 6.75** | 7.00** | - | - | - |
| V | 5.51** | 5.27** | 3.15** | - | - | - |
| VI | 5.60** | 5.66** | 5.90** | - | - | - |

df = 9
\* = significant at 0.05 level
\*\* = significant at 0.01 level

Looking at the data, increasing at a constant rate after the
intervention, it is not difficult to say with certainty that
the intervention and the Reality Therapy approach in the class
impacted students' scores on educational aspiration. The 't'
values also show significant difference between each pair of
observations between the pre-intervention and post-intervention
phases of the study. Graphs also show a steeprise showing
that the baseline and post-intervention data steadily increases.
Significant differences among baseline and post-intervention
data steadily increases. Significant differences among baseline observations and the increase in baseline data in the
expected direction of the post intervention scores make it
impossible to conclude anything against the impact of the
intervention. From all the available data one can easily
conclude that the intervention positively influenced the educational aspiration scores of the sample of students.

185

## Table No. 22

### Baroda High School

't' values of means of scores on Educational Aspiration scale on the various possible pairs of observations

| Observations | I | II | III | IV | V | VI |
|---|---|---|---|---|---|---|
| I | - | - | - | - | - | - |
| II | 1.03 | - | - | - | - | - |
| III | 3.05 | - | - | - | - | - |
| IV | 6.75** | 7.09** | 4.78** | - | - | - |
| V | 10.00** | 7.35** | 5.71** | 3.33** | - | - |
| VI | 9.45** | 10.00** | 6.53** | - | - | - |

df = 9
* = significant at 0.05 level
** = significant at 0.01 level

## Table No. 23

### M.G.M. School

t values of means of scores of Educational Aspiration Scale on various possible pairs of observations.

| Observation | I | II | III | IV | V | VI |
|---|---|---|---|---|---|---|
| I | - | - | - | - | - | - |
| II | - | - | - | - | - | - |
| III | 0.25 | 1.05 | - | - | - | - |
| IV | 5.38** | 5.18** | 8.00** | - | - | - |
| V | 6.00** | 8.01** | 6.04** | - | - | - |
| VI | 6.01** | 8.26** | 9.44** | - | - | - |

df = 9
* = significant at 0.05 level
** = significant at 0.01 level

Means of scores of Edu. Aspiration
plotted against the six observations

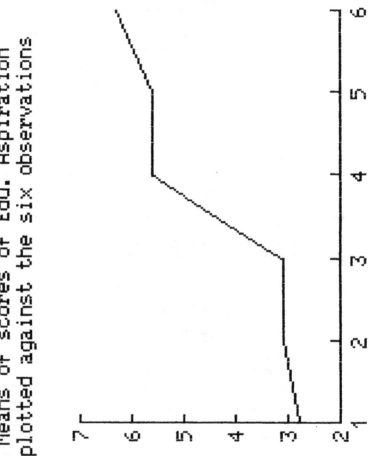

Means of Scores

Observations

M.G.M. SCHOOL

Means of scores of Edu. Aspiration
plotted against the six observations

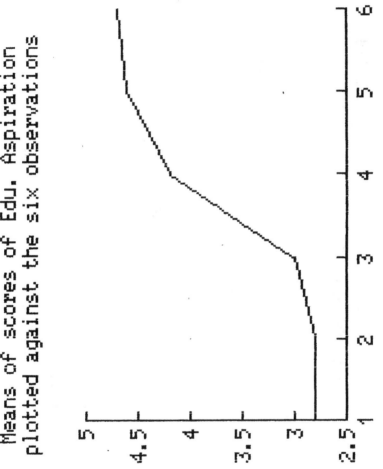

Observations

Means of Scores

Means of scores of Edu. Aspiration
plotted against the six observations

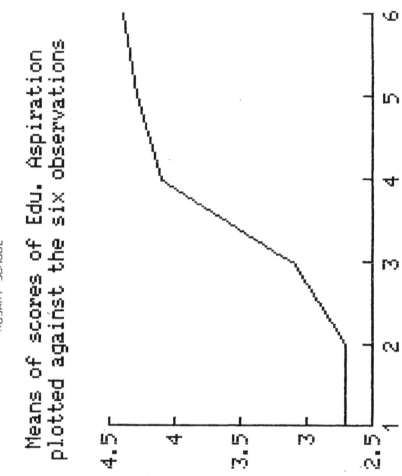

Means of Scores

Observations

187

## 5.5  Academic Achievement :

By Academic Achievement is meant how will students were
doing in their subjects of study as are required by the
syllabus. The percentages of students' aggregate grade points
averages on the different tests before and after the intervention were considered as indicators of academic performance.
The Means, standard Deviations of the six tests three before
and three after the intervention were presented in Table No.
(25) (26) and (27). The means of scores on pre- and post-
intervention observation clearly showed two distinct level of
magnitude. From this finding one may conclude that the
Intervention and the Reality Therapy Approach has had some
effect on the selected groups of students given in the tables
No. (28) (29) and (30) are the calculated 't' values of the
various possible pairs of observations. The tables show that
the post intervention observations significantly differed
from those of pre-intervention measures. Thus it may be
concluded that the significant departure of post-intervention
means from the means of the baseline series of observations
may be due to the impact of the intervention.

Graphs (13) (14) and (15) present the results visually
The steep slope in the line graphs was indicative of the
two distinct levels of magnitude in the pre and post intervention means. The data paths take a jump in the post-intervention phase and maintain a higher magnitude. It may be
concluded from the finding that the intervention and the
Reality Therapy approach have had a positive effect on the
students' academic. performance.

188

### Table No. 25

#### Baroda High School

Means, standard Deviations of the Academic Achievement Scale on the six observations.

| Observation | Mean | Standard Deviation |
| --- | --- | --- |
| 01 | 38.1 | 6.50 |
| 02 | 39.7 | 6.28 |
| 03 | 39.8 | 4.73 |
| Intervention . . . . . . . . . . . . . . . . . . . . . | | |
| 04 | 55.4 | 5.99 |
| 05 | 56.0 | 5.92 |
| 06 | 57.0 | 6.50 |

### Table No. 26

#### M. G. M. School

Means, standard deviations of Academic Achievement Scale on the six observations

| Observation | Mean | Standard Deviation |
| --- | --- | --- |
| 01 | 27.6 | 4.06 |
| 02 | 26.5 | 4.08 |
| 03 | 27.2 | 4.04 |
| Intervention . . . . . . . . . . . . . . . . . . . . | | |
| 04 | 42.3 | 3.35 |
| 05 | 44.7 | 4.00 |
| 06 | 46.3 | 2.57 |

Table No.27

Rosary School

Means, standard Deviations of the Academic Achievement
Scale on the six Observations

| Observation | Mean | Standard Deviation |
|---|---|---|
| 01 | 24.6 | 4.11 |
| 02 | 29.1 | 6.17 |
| 03 | 30.9 | 6.43 |
| Intervention . . . . . . . . . . . . . . . . . . . . . . | | |
| 04 | 38.1 | 2.59 |
| 05 | 41.8 | 1.53 |
| 06 | 41.9 | 2.55 |

Table No.28

Baroda High School

't' values of means of scores on Academic Achievement Scale
on various possible pairs of observations

| Observation | I | II | III | IV | V | V |
|---|---|---|---|---|---|---|
| I | - | - | - | - | - | - |
| II | 2.96 | - | - | - | - | - |
| III | 1.66 | 0.01 | - | - | - | - |
| IV | 10.01** | 8.48** | 10.06** | - | - | - |
| V | 9.83** | 7.39** | 8.43** | - | - | - |
| VI | 8.59** | 6.62** | 7.28** | - | - | - |

df = 9
* = significant at 0.05 level
** = significant at 0.01 level

## Table No.29

### M.G.M. School

't' values of means of scores on Academic Achievement Scale on various possible pairs of observations

| Observation | I | II | III | IV | V | VI |
|---|---|---|---|---|---|---|
| I | - | - | - | - | - | - |
| II | - | - | - | - | - | - |
| III | - | - | - | - | - | - |
| IV | 10.06** | 11.44** | 10.86** | - | - | - |
| V | 15.01** | 13.01** | 13.56** | - | - | - |
| VI | 18.01** | 18.00** | 17.00** | - | - | - |

df = 9
* = significant at 0.05 level
** = significant at 0.01 level

## Table No.30

### Rosary School

't' values of means of scores of Academic Achievement Scale various possible pairs of observations

| Observations | I | II | III | IV | V | VI |
|---|---|---|---|---|---|---|
| I. | - | - | - | - | - | - |
| II. | 3.87* | - | - | - | - | - |
| III. | 4.34** | 4.59** | - | - | - | - |
| IV. | 11.08** | 5.42** | 5.07** | - | - | - |
| V. | 8.68** | 6.28** | 4.49** | - | - | - |
| VI. | 10.00* | 6.15** | 5.00** | - | - | - |

df = 9
* = significant at 0.05 level
** = significant at 0.01 level

Means of scores of Academic Achievement plotted against the six observations

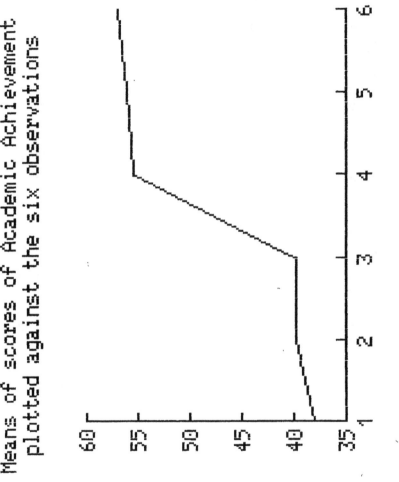

Observations

Means of Scores

Means of scores of Academic Achievement
plotted against the six observations

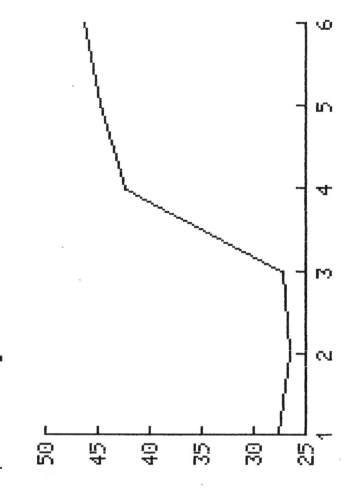

Means of Scores

Observations

Means of scores of Academic Achievement
plotted against the six observations

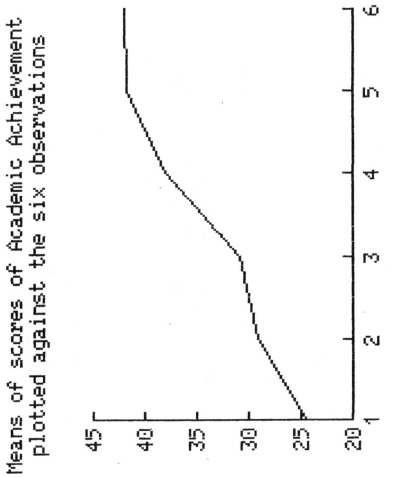

Means of Scores

Observations

## 5.6 Self-concept :

It refers to students' subjective feeling about what they are and what they consider their personal abilities and performance are. Here the students' self-concept was measured through Rosenberg's Society and Adolescent Self-Image Scale.

From the Data analyses it can be seen (Table No.31, 32 and 33) that there is sudden rise in the mean values immediately after the intervention. The 't' values also show that the pre and post-intervention means differ significantly from each other. The trend of change in the pre and post intervention series of observations was in the opposite direction. Those findings may tell of the possible impact of the intervention in raising the self-concept of the students. The different magnitudes of pre and post intervention means become even more vivid in graphical representations Plotted in graphs (16) (17) and (18) are the means of the six observations. The slope of the line graph is indicative of increase in the post-intervention scores one could note an increase in the post-intervention level from that of the pre-intervention as calculated from the means of both pre and post-intervention observations. This shows that the intervention programme affect the self-concept of the students positively.

Table No.31

Baroda High School

Means, standard Deviations of Self-concept Scale on
the Six Observations

| Observation | Mean | Standard Deviations |
|---|---|---|
| 01 | 2.4 | 0.49 |
| 02 | 2.6 | 0.49 |
| 03 | 3.0 | 0.63 |
| Intervention . . . . . . . . . . . . . . . . . . . . . . . | | |
| 04 | 5.6 | 0.92 |
| 05 | 6.1 | 0.70 |
| 06 | 5.7 | 1.10 |

Table No.32

M.G.M. School

Means, standard deviations of Self-concept Scale on
the Six observations.

| Observation | Mean | Standard deviation |
|---|---|---|
| 01 | 2.9 | 0.94 |
| 02 | 3.3 | 0.90 |
| 03 | 3.4 | 0.80 |
| Intervention . . . . . . . . . . . . . . . . . . . . . . . | | |
| 04 | 4.7 | 0.46 |
| 05 | 4.9 | 0.70 |
| 06 | 5.1 | 0.70 |

Table No.33

Rosary School

Means, standard deviations of the self-concept Scale
on the six observations

| Observation | Mean | Standard Deviation |
|---|---|---|
| 01 | 2.7 | 0.64 |
| 02 | 2.7 | 0.64 |
| 03 | 2.9 | 0.70 |
| Intervention . . . . . . . . . . . . . . . . . . . . . | | |
| 04 | 4.4 | 0.20 |
| 05 | 3.9 | 0.94 |
| 06 | 3.2 | 0.75 |

Table No.34

Baroda High School

't' values of means of scores on self-concept scale on the
various possible pairs of observations

| Observation | I | II | III | IV | V | VI |
|---|---|---|---|---|---|---|
| I. | - | - | - | - | - | - |
| II. | 1.5 | - | - | - | - | - |
| III. | 1.87 | 1.66 | - | - | - | - |
| IV. | 11.0** | 9.09** | 7.02** | | | |
| V. | 11.2** | 10.2** | 10.0** | 1.47 | - | - |
| VI. | 7.85** | 9.01** | 10.0** | - | - | - |

df  =  9
*   =  significant at 0.05 level
**  =  significant at 0.01 level

## Table No. 35

### M.G.M. School

't' values of means of scores on self-concept scale on various possible pairs of observations.

| Observation | I | II | III | IV | V | VI |
|---|---|---|---|---|---|---|
| I | - | - | - | - | - | - |
| II | - | - | - | - | - | - |
| III | 0.57 | 0.71 | - | - | - | - |
| IV | 8.18** | 7.75** | 7.64** | - | - | - |
| V | 5.56** | 5.16** | 7.14** | - | - | - |
| VI | 9.16** | 11.62** | 6.53** | - | - | - |

df = 9
\* = significant at 0.05 level
\*\* = significant at 0.01 level

## Table No. 36

### Rosary School

't' values of means of scores on Self-concept Scale on various possible pairs of observations

| Observation | I | II | III | IV | V | VI |
|---|---|---|---|---|---|---|
| I | - | - | - | - | - | - |
| II | - | - | - | - | - | - |
| III | 0.57 | 0.71 | - | - | - | - |
| IV | 5.50** | 5.66** | 5.84** | - | - | - |
| V | 4.08** | 3.52** | 4.66** | - | - | - |
| VI | 1.42 | 1.56 | 2.59** | - | - | - |

df = 9
\* = significant at 0.05 level
\*\* = significant at 0.01 level

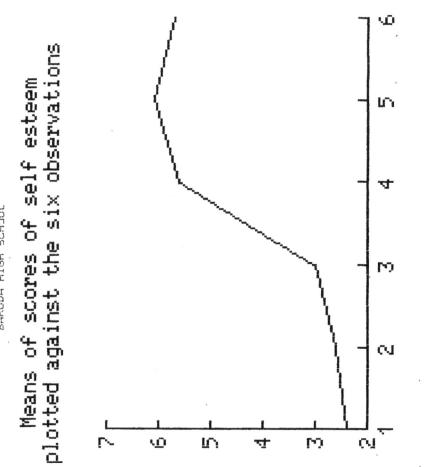

BARODA HIGH SCHOOL

Means of scores of self esteem
plotted against the six observations

Observations

Means of Scores

Means of scores of self esteem
plotted against the six observations

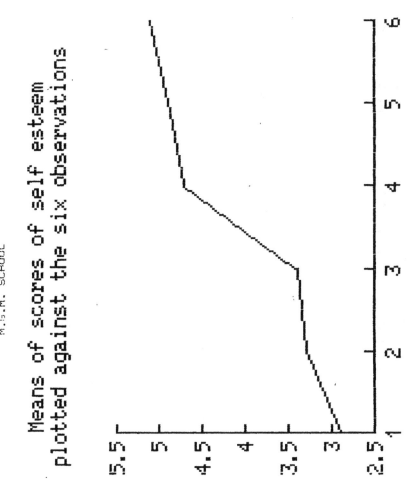

Observations

Means of Scores

Means of scores of self esteem
plotted against the six observations

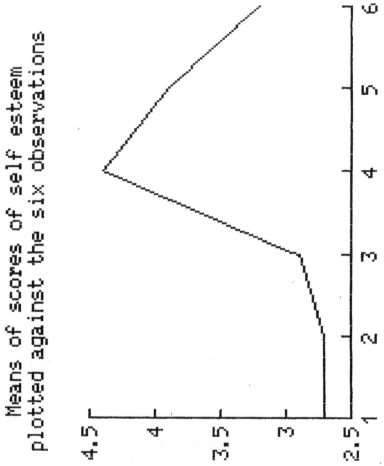

Observations

Means of Scores

## 5.7 Case Studies :

In order to discover in depth how the intervention programme based on Reality Therapy has made effect on the individual
students, six case studies, three representing students who
showed much gain, and three students who has not shown such
gain in the slected criterion variables were conducted. The
investigator had to prepare the case study report, depending on
the information acquired from class-room observation, anecdotal
record and from the personal interviews which were conducted
with the students and their parents. However the items of the
student interviews schedule and the the Parents' Interview
schedule were used as lead questions (Both of the Interview
schedules could be find in the Appendix ).

Basing on all those informations, a brief case report of
the above mentioned six students were prepared and is presented below. However, the six subjects, one high achiever and
one low achiever had been taken from each of the three groups
as representative of the whole group.

## 5.8 Case study -1

Student No.    - One
Age - 12 years  9 months

The student joined this present school in standard V. He
had studied in another school in another city  where his
father was doing business previously.

He has an younger brother and he has come from an affluent
business family. His father is a graduate and businessman and
his mother is a housewife who has studied upto Class IX., she
is a full time housewife.

The boy is quite intelligent and an observer would not
immediately notice the boy as a deviant. It was only after
spending three or four days in the class-room the investigator
started noticing that the boy is not fitting into the classroom norms. The student at first glance is like any other boy
in the class, slightly naughty but nothing particularly
unusual. However, as time went by, the investigator could
hear the boy's name from all sides.

The boy is constantly on the move in the classroom,
generally always teasing other students, whereas his own work
remains unfinished. As soon as the investigator assigned to
group some written works the student started his prowling
around. The pattern of events are invariably the same. After
writing a line or two he would feel like going to the toilet,
or sharpening his pencil or erasing something he has written
or suddenly he would feel that his pencil is small and without
any hesitation will grale someone's pencil. His lack of
concentration on the school tasks and his constant teasing of
other students made him unable to settle either with the
group tasks of adjust the peer group. Repeated efforts in
making him participate in the group works did not prove to be
very fruitful. The student would just look up at the investigator with a slight smile, swinging his feet all the while.
His attitude toward school also was not very positive, and it
seemed that he had no respect for the school teachers. On one
occassion it came out from him that teachers in his school
were concerned about money only and they did not have any

concern for the students. Consequently the student admitted
that only one or two hours are not enough for the study and
he felt that he himself is responsible for that, because he
gets all the amenities at home.. He also felt somewhat
responsible for his low academic achievement in school.

In the pre-intervention phase the student got considerable
low score in Attitude toward school, Educational Aspiration and
in Self-esteem. But in the Post-intervention phase he showed
marked progress in the above three variables and he was quite
happy with his progress. The improvement in those three
variables put a distinct mark on his achievement in school
subjects - and which brought parental satisfaction with their
ward immediately.

The intervention programme brought about changes in the
positive direction in his thinking acting and nearly every
aspect of life at school. He has more friends now, more
cooperative, has definite goals to be achieved and his grades
in the school showed marked improvement. During the interviews
with the investigator he expressed the fact that he himself
could observe the change in his thinking and behavior towards
others after the intervention programme, which has helped him
a lot with more self-confidence, self-esteem and optimism.
He is now a willing and active participant in several programmes
of the school. He has become more mature in his behavior. In
a word his whole attitude showed a significant change for the
better.

5.9  Case study - two

---

Student No.   :   Two

Age          :   13 years   3 months

---

The student of the case study is a plump boyish looking
girl with large eyes. For a long time almost one month after
the school had reopened one would find her sitting by herself
in a corner bench. Talking about the girl, the class-teacher,
strongly felt that she should not have been promoted to class-
IX at all. As the girl refused to talk or move from her bench
she did not have a single friend in the school. Comlaints to
parents about her were of no use. They did not even bother to
meet the class-teacher.

The girl's low score of attitude toward school was very
much indicative of her inability to come to terms with the
school tasks or the peer groups. Even when the investigator
asked about her personal things as to where she stayed, how
many brothers and sisters she  had or where she got her pretty
ribbon, the girl would simply refuse to respond. She just
looked up at the investigator looking scared. However the r
student is studying in this school from the beginning. In
fact before the  actual administration of the scales, the
investigator had to be friend the girl during the recess hours
Since she sat alone during the recess hours without moving
around, getting her to listen to something was not difficult.
Only after many sessions, the girl started responding with a
slight smile and in small sentences. However, her response
to the questions posed by the investigator were soft murmurs.

199

The girl and her family stayed in one room plus kitchen apartment. The house was situated on the third floor of an old building. She had younger brother and two younger sisters. She was the eldest among her brothers and sisters.

Her father was thirty-nine years old. He had studied only upto class Seven and was working as a truck driver. His working hours were quite long and his job left him tired and irritable. He did not have any free time to spare for his family or his wife. He was extremely short tempered and beat his wife and aughters frequently. The girl's mothers was thirty-two years old and had studied upto class five. She contributed to the family income by stitching Sari falls. Although she did not have to go out to work, she remained busy throughout the day. The household work was mainly done by daughters. They managed the cooking, cleaning and washing every day a l ongwith their school studies.

The family interactions as such appeared to be minimal, and it was generally restricted to the functional tasks alone. For her visits to the zoo, garden, cinema etc. were extremely rare. Toys or books were never part of her life.

However, in school, she considered herself a failure. She had failed in her school annual tests three times and according her opinion, as she was not at all a good student, so that nobody wanted to make friendship with her and the teachers often insulted her without any sufficient reason.

She usually studied two hours approximately every day, though she felt that she should give more effort to her study. But as she had to do a lots of housework she simply could not afford more time. She also was not well adjusted in her family.

Instead of all her disadvantages, she wanted to appear as
a good student in the eyes of her teachers, as well as her
class-mates. She was also much eager to have good relation
with her family members.

The girl's educational aspiration was not very high and
the investigator felt that it was mostly due to her low socio-
economic status. She wanted to be a professional fashion
designer or an efficient tailor just after passing school
leaving examination.

The pre-intervention tests showed that the girl has low
self-esteem, less assertive behavior and lacked high educational
aspiration.

But the post intervention tests showed that she became
more assertive and her sense of self esteem improved a great
deal. After the intervention programme the student's social
behavior revealed marked changes in the positive direction.
She has become more cheerful and is a better performer than
before. She become a good mixer and came out of her shell of
isolation. Her grades in studies showed marked improvement.
She gained self confidence and showed a confidant attitude
towards school work and her teachers. Her behaviour towards
her friends became more cordial and pleasant. Her attitude
towards life in general became more positive and she actively
started participating in school programme willingly and with
genuine interest.

5.10 <u>Case study - Three</u> :

---
student No.  :   Three
Age          :   13 years
---

The student joined the present school in standard II. He had come from a middle class educated family.

The father was 42 years old. He had a graduate degree in commerce and he was the Regional Transport Officer. His office hours were from 9.30 a.m. to 5.30 p.m. In the evening he was back at home at about 6 o'clock. He generally spent the evening hours with his friends, outside the house, playing carom or chit-chating with them.

The mother was 37 years old and had done her nursing course from England. But at present she was not working anywhere, just looking after the family.

The boy stated in a concrete roofed three roomed apartment with his father, mother, younger brothers parental grand parents, parental aunt and a parental uncle.

The investigator had close rapoort with the student and it gradually came out through conversations that the family members did not devote much time to him. They not only didnot talk to him much but also didnot listen to what he had to say.

The student's academic performance was just average and he had mixed attitude toward school positive as well as negative.

At school, he was lonely had not many friends and also felt distance from the teachers. He lacked self-confidence and often mummbled while giving answer in the class.

However at home too he had few friends of his own age group. The home being in a predominantly Muslim locality and on the main road where there was heavy flow of traffic, the boy was not allowed to go and play outside. Therefore his participation in physcial activities and his interaction with his peers was extremely limited. He studied 3 to 4 hours everyday on average and thought it was enough for preparing school works, though he was not at all satisfied with his school results and wanted to get much higher marks than what he was getting at present.

During the group sessions the investigator made the student aware of the fact that only nursing ambition was not enough. Ambition without hard work brought only frustration. The investigator also discovered some of his personal qualities during the sessions and helped him to develop them.

The pre-intervention tests showed that the student got low score in self-esteem, assertiveness and in the sense of responsibility. But after the intervention programme the student developed more confidence and a sense of belongingness to the school. His social behavior changed for the better and his academic grades showed significant improvement. He started taking a willing and very active share in the school activities. He gradually became much more helpful and responsible. What perhaps the student learnt to relate to others in general had its impact in the classroom and also at home. During the personal interviews he opined that he liked

the group sessions very well. He reported a that it helped
him to discover his qualities understand himself better
improve communication and relationship with others. He remarked
that knowing his qualities made him to think good about him.
He also said that the intervention programme helped him to make
more friends. It was evident that his self-confidence increased. He also experienced life to be more happy and thus have
more energy for study and other activities at home and at
school.

5.11 Case Study - Four :

---

| | | |
|---|---|---|
| Student No. | : | Four |
| Age | : | 13 years  5   months |

---

The student is in the school from the nursery class and
she has come from a middle class family. She has one elder
sister and she is the youngest daughter in the family and
much pampered by the family members. Her father is graduate
and working in a responsible position and  her mother is a
house-wife who had passed only school leaving examination.

The student was good in studies in the early days of her
school but for the last four five years she is showing a
marked deterioration, though her attitude toward school is
quite positive. She admitted that she has some problems in
the school often she had problems in understanding subjects
or in explaining things while giving answers either oral or
written.

. The investigator observed that the girl is of average intelligence but her deterioration in studies only made her back benchers. The girl works for her school subjects two hours daily on average. However she felt that this is not enough for making progress.

The parents as well as the teachers thought that the girl is lazy and often the parents had to be after her to make her study more.

The pre-intervention tests showed that the student scored low in sense of responsibility, educational aspiration as well as in self-esteem. She is also not confident about her abilities. The intervention programme do not produce any noticeable changes in her performance.

She is still lagging behind in studies, managing to get through the sybjects. In the school she hardly participated in class or school activities. She does not answer correctly to most of the questions put to her in the class. She has no stable relationship with any class mates and she is one of the least accepted in the class. The student confessed that she did not take the group sessions seriously and she did not really attempted to do anything about her difficulties and continued to be victimized by others.

Though endowed with ability to pursue academic studies successfully, she does not show sufficient interest in any of the school activities. She never expresees herself freely or cheerfully in any of the conversation with her school mates. She is not convinced about the value of her participation in the intervention programme. She expressed the view that the programme has not effected any positive change in her thinking and activities.

## 5.12 Case study - Five :

| | | |
|---|---|---|
| Student No. | : | Five |
| Age | : | 13 years  2 months |

He is a thin boy usually quiet and timid in the class. He does not mingle much with the other students. During the intervention session the student was not one of the active outgoing one rarely raised his hand or answered the investigator's queries enthusiastically. The boys father workes as a worker in one of the local industries. He had passed his intermediate. He does not have any particular hobby or interest and his interactions with the children are extremely limited. The boy's mother is an young lady who had her scholling till class seven. She is a full time housewife. In general, the family atmosphere seemed to be tense and there is not much harmony or cohesion amongst the family members. Lack of finance, limited parental education and limited interest in the family made the interaction within it very restrictive. The family is unconcerned about the boy's participation intervention programme and the parental interest was confined merely to the progress card brought home.

However in the post-intervention phase no perceptible desirable change in the behavior has been observed. His educational performance does not show any improvement as a result of the intervention programme. For him there is no clear educational goal. For the student himself study is not so important. He does not have any regular study hours either and which he skips at the sligh-test of excuse. His self-esteem score is also poor. In short the intervention programme

has not made any difference to him as a person and as a
student in his studies.

5.13  Case study - Six :

| | | |
|---|---|---|
| Student No. | : | Six |
| Age | : | 13 years  4 months |

He is a good looking boy with lovely sparkling eyes. He
is like a butterfly fluttering around in the classroom. Even
when the rest of the class is engaged in one task or the other,
the boy would be find moving around in the classroom by
disturbing other students. During the initial days of the
intervention the investigator tried to make him participate in
the class-room activity but there is no improvement. The boy
follows no school or classroom norms and hardly ever does
the home assignment. His low score in attitude toward school
is very much indicative of his inability to settle down with
the school routine. His academic score is also very low. He
is simply not interested in school and moreover he is not
afraid of anything. Hence no amount of suggestions and
persuasions worked with him. The investigator felt that his
home is responsible for his absolute indifference to school.

His father is a 35 years old businessman. He had completed his secondary schooling and remains very busy with his
work. His involvement in the household matter is very limited.

The mother is a young housewife. The boy is her first
child. She had studied upto class IX. Both of the parents
did not have any interest in books or magazines. The boy is
given a lot of freedom by the parents. He is hardly ever
restricted in what he did. As such he does exactly what he
wants during the day. At home neither of the parents super-
vised his home work. Wherever he requires anything he just
had to ask for money. The parents did not have to bother
about anything at all.

In the post intervention phase the student informed to
the investigator that he had very little faith in the effect
of the programme. His social behavior does not reveal change
in the positive direction. He failed to develop a more
positive attitude towards his classmates, teachers and works
at school. The programme has very little effect on his
attitude or behavior. After the intervention programme he
did not show significant improvement in any of the criterion
variables perhaps a more intensive programme of this nature
may be required for such students.

## 5.14 An overview of the case studies :

The first three case studies given above represent
students who did well in the selected criterion variables, and
the last three case studies are of students who did not do so
well in them. While giving description of the six homes a more
or less clear pattern emerged. A discussion of these six
cases showed that complete negligence of the child's needs by
parents due to whatever reason, stood out to be the single
most important factor that affected the child both in academic
achievement as well as in personality characteristics. This
was clearly observed in all the six cases. Parental negligence

and parental preoccupation showed their effects in different
aspects and spheres of home life. The tensions at home and
lack of a conducive and caring home breed a certain negative
characteristics in the child and he thus was unable to adjust
to school demands or peer groups. This in turn made them more
withdrawn and lonely. They were unable to perform well in the
school tests which in turn upsets them as well as the parents.
Thus the whole turn of events continued to deteriorate.

Again, in the present study caution essentially should be
exercised in highlighting the importance of school adjustment.
In fact the teaching learning processes, as well as the evaluation procedures adopted by the schools were much against the
desirable learning strategies advocated by psychologists and
educationists for the present age group. If one could indulge
in a bit of subjective observations, one could say that these
six children were mere puppets at school. They seldom showed
normal curiosity, exuberance and creativity which theoretically
the twelve or thirteen years old were supposed to exhibit.

A popular write up on Indian education in a daily news-
paper by a leading Indian educationist sarcastically sums up
the scenario of the Indian education. According to him,"Indian
school is a recipe for intellectual genocide centered in text-
books, its deadly burden and indifference to children's personality gets combined with insensitive teaching in ill equipped
classrooms." (Krishna kumar 1990).

Therefore, any interpretation made of the academic achievement or adjustment to school should essentially be made,
keeping in consideration to the prevailing classroom conditions.

However, this unsuitable and negative family and school situation could be greatly redeemed if an anchor of some sort is there, for the child. Probably a therapeutic counsellor could help these children a great deal and this had been proved to be true in the case of three high achievers who in spite of their difficulties at home and in school improved a great deal.

The investigator, however did not consider the low achievers as lost cases. May be their problems were more deep seated and only more close associations with them, by using the techniques of Reality Therapy could help them in the long run.

## 5.15 Discussion :

The quantitative analyses have revealed that the Reality Therapy Intervention programme has effected significant improvement in the selected criterion variables. Results showed that there has been marked gains in assertiveness, educational aspiration, sense of responsibility, self-esteem, attitude toward school and academic achievement.

The qualitative analysis attempted here is done with a view to interpret and find meaning to the changes brought about in the external behavior of the individual student and the development or effect within the individual person.

The present discussion avoids making any one to one correspondence between the observed student gains on the specified criterion variables and their cause. The investigator considers reality to be a matrix of the inter-relationships between several forces that are at work within the

individual student. Therefore what is observed it is assumed
is the combined impact of the facilitative dimensions provided
by the investigator and the students enhanced awareness of
their own abilities.

The findings of the study showed that the growth of all
the variables mentioned about in the post-intervention phase
of the study was significant either at 0.05 or 0.01 level.
This was corroborated by the analysis of data gathered from
the interviews with the students. There was an overall
increase of hours in the amount of time spent on personal study
Twenty seven students out of the total thirty, have positive
liking for the school and in the opinion of the students they
are feeling more confident, optimist about future and assertive in their day to day dealing with others. Similarly the
intervention has a significant impact on enhancing students
sense of responsibility (viz. table of responsibility) The
post-intervention observation showed better attitude toward
school than before (viz. table of attitude toward school).
Therefore one can easily conclude to the positive contribution
of the Reality Therapy programme from the findings observed,
although there is difference in the scores from school to
school. Baroda High School scored highest in all the variables,
M.G.M. school has somewhat low scores than the previous one,
while keeping the Rosary School in the last position. The observed
findings may have been the effect of the difference in the
climate created by the school authority. Though according to
the students' own rating nearly all the participants improved
themselves in all the variables in the post-intervention phase.
The statistical tables and graphs confirmed more or less the
above findings

Following Carl Roger's we can say that the basic nature of the human being when functioning freely is constructive and trustworthy    that is, when we are able to free the individual from defensiveness he is open to the wide range of his own needs as well as the wide range of environmental and social demands, his reactions may be trusted to be positive forward moving and constructive. (Rogers, 1980).

The same observations were made by the investigator in the process of growth that had taken place in the intervention period among the students with whom she had the facility to work closely. It was not merely an opportunity of having to work hand in hand with them for an external use - indeed it was far beyond that. It was an opportunity to see life open up, blossom and grow. Especially through the opportunity of having been with the three groups of school youths, following them up through a developmental course for a full academic session and beyond that, closely following their internal frame of mind, entering into the underlying tone of their spontaneous responses, personal sharing, the investigator has come to realize how much the youth had a need today of having caring teachers who will be their friend and facilitators in bringing about a transformation of hope and confidence in the lives of the youths, causing the youths to rise and aim at meaningful goals for life.

The rapport or warmth and unconditional respect toward each individual student which the investigator tried to communicate created a reciprocal response from the participants. It was a continuous experience of the investigator in the three groups that the students accepted her as one of their friends. They were uninhibited by her presence in the group when it came to personal sharing and opening up. The integrative atmosphere in the classroom provided opportunity to pupils to feel free and to participate actively in the class. Free and spontaneous actions were clearly perceived on the part of the pupils who never used to speak in the class. Communication had improved as they were confident enough to voice their thoughts. They were able to convince and dealt with people, learnt to x identify and more importantly admitted their mistakes. The students became more curious and a urge was developed in them to know more than the routine information about the topic of learning. Some students were assigned the responsibility of helping other pupils which they found challenging as they got more chance to exhibit their talents and abilities.

Students markedly exhibited closer relationships with their peer, teachers and showed more positive behaviors and liking towards their schools. Most of the students reduced fear and were more free to express their ideas and feelings. There was a noticeable positive change in the students especially those with problem behaviors. Those pupils happened to get not only accepted but they themselves got more involved in the classroom activities. Before the intervention programme most of the pupils did not have clear perception about their abilities and attitudes. But the intervention programme increased their confidence and indirectly the programme helped to improve their performance. Pupils liked the period for group work. It created awareness about their own interests and abilities. It was found that even the isolated pupils involved themselves in the programme and worked enthusiastically. Pupils began to suggest their own plans for new activities. About the goal setting behavior, it was observed that the gap was more between goal supposition and goal obtained. Within the intervention programme a definitely positive change

was perceived in their behavior. The students began setting
more realistic goals according to their self expectation and
worked harder to achieve the goal supposed, considering it as
a commitment on their part to do so. The participants had
special thrill in doing the exercises which brought out the
prescribed message. One of the reasons for this was that it
was a group exercise. Since the larger group of the class was
turned into smaller group during the intervention programme,
the participants experienced a greater freedom, closeness,
trust and a sense of excitement and healthy competitibn which
induced them to bring out the best in them. Some of the
participants have reported that their experiential learning
had been very powerful through the presentation of exercises
during the intervention programme. The students who had gone
through the course had reported that they  had been rejuvenated
with a new life because of the experiences they have had.

The investigator felt the thrill of it even more exqui-
sitely. Such an experience of being with the youth and watch-
ing the process of an onward growth in them had enriched her
own life. The investigator to some extent had tried to
resonate  with the aspirations, disappointments and even
moments of frustration expressed by the students.

It was not easy to assess the impact of a programme such
as this. Teachers of the school responded positively and the
general atmosphere had been supportive of the programme's
development. Parents also seemed to be aware of the purpose
and nature of the programm.

However throughout the programme the investigator gathered lots of information from the students to help in the
programme's development. The information which the investigator collected only proved that the students supported the
basic concepts of Reality Therapy.

The students admitted repeatedly that it was very hard
for them to establish goals and to develop proper learning
activity or to get rid of bad habits because of their inexpe-
rience in doing such work but this was the first time that
they had ever been able to reach beyond a certain point, no
matter how hard they had tried in the past. The students also
emphasised that it was unfortunate that they had not this kind
of opportunity until their senior year.

But note of disharmony was not wanting. All the students
who underwent the Reality Therapy Intervention programme did
not show the same desirable positive change in behavior.
Perhaps an intensive programme of this nature may be required
for such students.

However all the problems appeared to have a reasonable
solution and it went without saying that the basic concepts
of Reality Therapy proved to be an excellent way to introduce
much needed innovation in traditional system without sacrifi-
cing quality or quantity of the school's existing educational
system.

## CHAPTER : VI

## SUMMARY AND CONCLUSION

### 6.1 Introduction :-

The present study is on Reality Therapy - introduced by
Dr. William Glasser is a psychological education programme.
Dr. Glasser's approach is fairly straight forward one, which
places confidence in the teacher's ability to deal with his/her
students' needs through a realistic or rational process.
Reality Therapy is simply a special kind of teaching or training
programme which attempts to teach a student what he should have
learned during his normal growth in a rather short period of
time.

Glasser and his collaborator Zunin (1970) suggested that
Reality Therapy is applicable to students with behaviour and
learning problems as well as to any individual student or group
of students seeking either to gain a successful identity for
themselves and/or to help others toward this same goal.

Focusing on the present behaviour, the teacher guides the
student to enable him to see himself accurately, to face reality,
to fulfill his own needs without harming himself or others. The
crux of this theory is personal responsibility for one's own
behaviour.

Easy or difficult as its application may be in any particular case, the specialized learning situation which Glasser
calls Reality Therapy is made up of three seperate but intimately
interwoven phases.

(a)  First there will be the involvement. The therapist must
     become so involved with the students, that the student
     will begin to face reality and see how his behaviour is
     unrealistic.

(b)  The therapist must reject the behavior which is unrealistic
     but still accept the student and maintain his involvement
     with him.

(c)  The therapist must teach the student responsible ways to
     to fulfill his needs within the confines of reality.

Usually the most difficult phase of Reality Therapy is the
first, i.e. the gaining of the involvement - a completely
honest human relationship in which the student perhaps for the
first time in his life realizes that someone cares enough
about him, not only to accept him but to help him fulfill his
needs in the real world. The ability of the therapist to get
involved is the major skill of doing Reality Therapy.

Once the involvement occurs the therapist begins to
insist that the student should face the reality of his
behavior. The therapist no longer allows the student to evade
recognizing what he is doing or his responsibility for it.

When the therapist takes these above mentioned steps the
relationships deepns, because now someone cares enough about
the student to make him face a truth that he has spent his
life trying to avoid it - i.e. he himself is responsible for
his behavior. No reason is acceptable to the therapist for
any irresponsible behavior. He confronts the student with
his behavior and asks him to decide whether or not he is taking
the responsible course.

217

As the part of becoming involved the therapist must become
interested in and discuss all aspects of the student's present
life.  The therapist must be interested in him as a person with
a wide potential not just as a student with problems.  The
therapist must open up his life, talk about new horizons expand
his range of interest make him aware of life beyond his difficulties.  Thus the student develops an increased sense of self-
worth in the process of parrying his convictions and values
with a trusted respected person.  The therapist now directly
but skillfully interweave a discussion of the student's strong
points, discussing those areas in which the student acts
responsibly and shows how they can be expanded.  Responsibility
is a very important concept in Reality Therapy and it is
defined in this therapy as the ability to fulfill one's needs.

Because the student must gain responsibility right now
the therapist should always focus on the present.  The past has
certainly contributed to what he is now,  but we cannot change
the past, only the present.  Recounting his history in the
hope that he will learn from his mistakes rarely proves successful and should be avoided.  Excuses for deviant behavior are
not accepted and one's history can't be more important than
one's present life.  The therapist never blames others for the
student's irresponsibility such as mother, father or anyone
deeply involved with the student no matter how irresponsible
they are or were.  The student can't change them, he can only
learn better ways to live with them or without them.

In Reality Therapy therefore the therapist rarely asks why ?
His unusual question is "What are you doing ?" and not "Why are
you doing it ? "

When the student admits that his behavior is irresponsible
the last phase of therapy "Relearning" begins. Actually no
definite change in the therapy occurs relearning is merged
into the whole treatment. The student must rely on the therapist's experience to help him learn better ways of behavior.

It is only a matter of time untill the student with his
newly acquired responsible behavior begins to fulfill his needs.
He finds new relationships, more satisfying involvements, and
need the therapist less. Visits become less frequent as both
the therapist and the student get aware of the approaching end.
But it is not necessarily final nor should it be. The stress
and strain of living may cause the student to return but not
for more than brief relearning periods. Once the specific
situation is responsibily handled the student leaves the
therapy.

## 6.2 Rationale for the present study :

The psychological orientation in education is fast developing as a powerful alternative to our present system of education. Today it is emerging as a potent force in the schools
and colleges. The main purpose of Reality Therapy ( which is
nothing but a psychological educational programme ) is to use
the classroom as a means of promoting personal growth and development. Reality Therapy is nothing but a way of integrating
learning about oneself into education systematically - which
is an urgent need of the day. In a world that is changing so
fast our well being and effectiveness will depend on how well
we are able to relate communicate, understand ourselves and
others. Reality Therapy is a way to this goal. When the learning

climate is one of acceptance of the learner as he is and his
needs for 'security and self-esteem are satisfied, he can
explore new avenues of growth and drive for self-actualization.
Our present study Reality Therapy aims at helping the students
to reach this final end.

For the causes mentioned above the investigator has taken
the present study.

## 6.3 The Statement of the Problem :

"Preparation, try out and study of effectiveness of a
psychological education programme for High School students
based on William Glasser's Reality Therapy".

## 6.4 The concern of the present study :

The concern of the present study was to understand the
student in transition - the student which graduates out of
the relatively structured and familiar ethos of the school, to
the intervention programme of the Reality Therapy.

The demands that the intervention programme makes on the
students and the responses they make to those demands with all
their developmental characteristics and the support they get
from the programme itself and the investigator were all concern
of the present study.

The theoretical and practical aspects of Reality Therapy
provided a perspective in which one has to view the developing student and his/her, social, psychological context.

The study was initiated by formulating in precise terms
the objectives it sought to answer and they were the following

6.5  objectives of the study :-

    a)    To prepare a programme of psychological education
        based on William Glasser's Reality Therapy.

    b)    To study the effectiveness of Reality Therapy in
        bringing about changes in students with respect
        to the following major components of their academic
        as well as psychological development.

        ( a)  Assertiveness
        ( b)  Sense of Responsibility
        ( c)  Attitude toward school
        ( d)  Educational Aspiration
        ( e)  Academic Achievement
        ( f)  Self concept.

6.6  Hypotheses of the study :

In the light of the concept of Reality Therapy presented
earlier and the objectives stated above, the following Research
Hypotheses were generated regarding the effectiveness of the
Reality Therapy. Intervention programme. When the teacher
understands the students, when the students see themselves
accepted and valued, they begin to regain their lost powers
and as a result improve their academic performance, discover
their hidden talents, and thus become confident. This also
could bring about better cooperation with their peers and a
feeling of belongingness to the group. They develop positive
ways of looking at things around them and the learning experience thus turn out to be a satisfying one. The present study

attempts to test some of these hypotheses the following research hypotheses have been stated for the present study. Students behavior in respect of :-

a) Assertiveness
b) Sense of Responsibility
c) Attitude toward school
d) Educational Aspiration
e) Academic Achievement
f) Self concept.

before and after the intervention, orienting the group along a Reality Therapy perspective will differ.

## 6.7 The Sample :

The sample of the present study consisted of 30 students of class IX from three different schools of Baroda city, 10 students each from each school, who have been selected on the basis of learning or behavioural problems. The sample was selected keeping in mind the following criteria :-

### (a) School performance :

The students whose academic performance is generally low over the last three years. The past records of school performances also have been taken into consideration.

### (b) Disciplinary problems :

Students, who without any apparent/sufficient reason create disciplinary problems in the school.

(c) Opinions of the concerned teachers :

Opinions of the different teachers of class IX of the three schools, regarding the students' poor academic performance disciplinary problems have been taken.

(d) Personal and informal/interviews of the investigator with all students of class IX of the three schools, selected for carrying out the programme. The interviews were mostly related with questions regarding the students' home, school peer groups, aspirations, hobbies, interests etc. to draw out more first-hand information from the students themselves and thus to reach a concrete decision regarding the choice of students for the intervention programme.

## 6.8 The Design :

The present investigation is an intervention study and the approach is developmental in nature. The study aims at evaluating changes on the sample as a result of the intervention strategies employed. Therefore, the time series design is considered to be most apt for the purpose of the present study.

## 6.9 Intervention :

An intervention programme was prepared following the guidelines of Reality Therapy as given by Dr. William Glasser. were given to the students in the following three phases to enhance assertiveness sense of responsibility, positive attitude toward school, educational aspiration, academic achievement and self concept.

(a) 1st Phase - Involvement with the students, by creating a warm and supportive climate in the group.

(b) 2nd Phase - Knowledge about one's own unrealistic behavior and gradual avoidance of it.

(c) 3rd Phase - Relearning of Responsible ways to fulfill one's needs within the confines of Reality

6.10 Instruments :

In order to ascertain the effectiveness of Reality Therapy in fostering student growth on the variables specified under the objectives of the study, the following measurement tools were used.

a) Tasneem Naqvi's Assertiveness Scale.

b) A Responsibility Scale prepared by the Investigator.

c) Lawrence J. Dolan and Marci Morrow Eno's school Attitude Scale.

d) Nageswara Rao's Educational Aspiration Scale.

e) Academic Achievement in the various tests of class VIII and IX.

f) Rosenberg's Society and Adolescent's self Image Scale.

g) Interview schedule for students.

h) Interview schedule for parents.

i) Case studies.

j) An Anecdotal Record.

k)   The Educational Environment at Home Scale.

l)   The Home Interaction Pattern Scale.

m)   The Social Competence Scale.

n)   Behavioral Adjustment Inventory.


6.11 Data Collection :

For data collection the samples were administered the
research tools three times before orienting the samples along
the Reality Therapy Intervention programme in order to determine the status of the specified criterion variables. Again
after the intervention the samples were administered the same
set of tools three times to find out if there was any
significant difference in the measures. These observation
tools were taken with an interval of four weeks apart.

The Responsibility Scale was however administered only
twice in the pre-intervention phase though it was administered
three times after the intervention.

For measuring Academic Achievement a deliberate decision
was made not to go for standardised achievement tests, instead
teacher made tests were made use of the decision was taken
since academic achievement as a variable in the hypothesised
causal model represented more the conformity of the child to
the academic expectation of the given school milieu and less
an indicator of the scholastic abilities of the child defined
in absolute terms. Percentage of marks secured by the students
in the various test of class VIII and IX were taken as criteria
for determining academic achievement in the pre and post
intervention phase.

Once during the pre intervention phase and once during
the post intervention phase each student was interviewed
individually to get more information about them. The interview schedule for the parents were sent to them through their
wards to know their opinions regarding the improvement of
their children and after the programmes.

For case studies six students were chosen to study indepth. Their choice was done applying the following criteria
one student from each group who gained a great deal in all
crierion measures like self-esteem Educational aspiration,
Academic Achievement, Assertiveness Positive attitude toward
school sense of Responsibility and in the overall judgement
of the investigator which she arrived at, as a result of her
months of observations and interaction with them during the
experimentation period and during the interviews. Similarly
one student from each group was identified from among those
who did not well in the above criteria. Basing on all the
pieces of information the investigator made a brief report
on each of the six students. An Anecdotal record was kept
by the investigator throughout the whole programme. Again,
Interview Schedule for students and parents, The Educational
Environment at home scale, The Home Interaction Pattern Scale,
The social competence scale, Behavioral Adjustment Inventory
were all used to get more ideas about the students and thus
to prepare case histories observation report in general of
the programme in the proper limelight.

## 6.12 Data Analysis :

The data thus collected being both quantitative and qualitative were subjected to both quantitative and qualitative analyses. For quantitative data, means, standard deviations of each variable of all the six observations were computed. Again t-tests were conducted to determine the levels of difference among successive data points, seperated by different time intervals in the series. The data were then transformed into line graphs using means of observation were plotted over different intervention phases.

For qualitative data the group processes during the intervention programme were recorded in detail without using any structured observation schedule classroom incidents as they ocurred were faithfully recorded using anecdotal recording technique. Six children were selected for case studies on the bases of their achievement on the selected variables. Three of them were high achievers and three low achievers. Unstructured interviews were conducted with those students and through a series of scales and inventory administration, case study reports were prepared for each of these six children.

The experience of the investigator in the process have been varied and enriching. The psychological education programme using Reality Therapy awakened in the students an awareness of their own identities, potentialities a vision of their life goals, and a striving to attain their realization, now while at school and steadily thereafter in the future.

All of these will lead them to live an abundant life blossoming into growth and well-being.

The findings of the present study once again emphasized that for the development of the whole person, there is a need to supply teachers who are trained in psychological education and who could adopt facilitative teacher behaviors and promote the total growth of the students, both affective and cognitive. Such an education only could help to develop students unique potentialities by integrating both their ideas mind and feelings and learn to get along with human race with compassion and love.

As the goal of psychological education and Reality Therapy is to produce self actualizing and fully functioning individuals who can feel for others, training on such whole person model becomes imperative.

To reach this end, students affective needs should be given atleast as much consideration as their cognitive needs. No person can truly live effectively in a more coherent way with other human beings if he lacks either the necessary cognitive or affective skills

## 6.13 Major findings :

The following is a summary of the major findings of the study :-

Reality Therapy helped to enhance interpersonal relation-ships among students in the group.

a)  Students showed significant improvement in asserti-veness.

b)  Students' sense of responsibility also improved

c)  Students positive attitude toward school was enhanced.

d)  Students' educational aspiration improved considerably.

e)  Students showed marked improvement in Academic Achievement.

f)  Students' growth on self concept was positive.

However, the degree of improvement varied from group. to group. Whereas Baroda High School showed marked improvement in all the variables, the students of Rosary School did not show much improvement. MGM School's position in improvement was however in the middle.

The difference in improvement could be lent to the facts to the particular school's co-operation, availability of working days and due to some preconceived misconception about psychological education. among students teachers and the management of the school in general.

## 6.14 Implication for Further Research :

The present study attempts to achieve a balanced blend of quantitative and qualitative approaches. However, this should be taken just as the essential first step towards construucting a wholistic reality about the student in transition during the intervention period. The study reveals the possibility of further steps both in the quantitative and qualitative directions.

The quantitative part of the present study generates an empirically verified model of causal links among selected variables. The present attemot was focussed on a sample of limited size. One could articulate a larger samole and empirically verify it to derive stable indicators of causal relationships.

Student is an evolving phenomenon. Certain tendencies revealed in the present study therefore will get consolidated and certain others altered, as the student progresses through his schooling. A multi-cross sectional survey and a path analysis on its basis will be greatly useful in understanding the student as a growing entity, a little better.

The qualitative part of the study can perhaps be followed up with more intensive observations, and interviews making greater use of phenomenological and ethnological approaches. Also, on the basis of case studies attempted here, more elements could be brought to greater scruting in the future studies. Similarly, certain crucial processes and inter-actions at home and greater details in such studies.

CPSIA information can be obtained
at www.ICGtesting.com
Printed in the USA
LVHW042109310323
743153LV00020B/351